# GOLFING IN
# HEELS

# GOLFING IN HEELS

*What* MEN KNOW About Golf
That WOMEN NEED to Master in Life

## KIRSTEN FLORY

*Golfing in Heels*
Copyright © 2020 by Kirsten Flory.

All rights reserved. No part of this publication may be reproduced, distributed, or transmitted in any form or by any means, including photocopying, recording, or other electronic or mechanical methods, without the prior written permission of the copyright holder, except in the case of brief quotations embodied in critical reviews and certain other noncommercial uses permitted by copyright law. For permission requests, write to the publisher, addressed "Attention: Permissions Coordinator," at the address below.

ISBN: Soft Cover – 978-1-64318-055-7

Imperium Publishing
1097 N. 400th Rd
Baldwin City, KS, 66006

www.imperiumpublishing.com

# *Table of Contents*

Acknowledgements. . . . . . . . . . . . . . . . . . . . . . . . . . . vii
Introduction. . . . . . . . . . . . . . . . . . . . . . . . . . . . . . . . . .ix
Golf is Not Just a Man's Game . . . . . . . . . . . . . . . . . . . 15
I am Not a Golfer. . . . . . . . . . . . . . . . . . . . . . . . . . . . . 39
Finding the (Cart) Path . . . . . . . . . . . . . . . . . . . . . . . 59
Gimme Gimme . . . . . . . . . . . . . . . . . . . . . . . . . . . . . 73
Who's Your Caddy? . . . . . . . . . . . . . . . . . . . . . . . . . . 87
Drive . . . . . . . . . . . . . . . . . . . . . . . . . . . . . . . . . . . . . . 99
Conquering Fear . . . . . . . . . . . . . . . . . . . . . . . . . . . 111
Whiff. . . . . . . . . . . . . . . . . . . . . . . . . . . . . . . . . . . . 123
The Back Nine . . . . . . . . . . . . . . . . . . . . . . . . . . . . 127
Power Play . . . . . . . . . . . . . . . . . . . . . . . . . . . . . . . 133

# *Acknowledgements*

THIS BOOK IS dedicated to all of the women who thought "why not?" and those that took the leap to get in the game.

**GOLFING IN HEELS**

# *Introduction*

**MY FIRST EXPERIENCE** with golf was at a YMCA golf clinic for kids when I was in my early teens. I hated it. I had to drag around a heavy bag of clubs for the afternoon and felt like I was not making any progress or sense whatsoever. I didn't touch a golf club, nor set foot on a golf course after that, for many many years.

Fast forward to life for me in college. I worked full time to pay rent and other expenses, in addition to taking a full load of classes. I started college as a biology major fully intending to make myself a pre-med student. Boy was I wrong. I failed with a big fat "F" an organic chemistry lecture in the second semester of my freshman year. I had never failed a class in my life. It was derailing, to say the least. It was a pivot point in my young life, an opportunity to take stock of what I was really good at. College was frustrating to me, trying to not only figure out what I wanted to pursue as a career, but what made sense as a degree (and quite honestly - how I can graduate in the shortest amount of time without racking up an extreme amount of debt). I had a good conversation with my parents during this time, and my mom asked me something that stuck with me. She asked me what classes that I took in high school did I really enjoyed? What made me come alive when I was part of it?

The answer? I did a lot of things in high school. I was in the marching band. I was an athlete. I was an excellent student grade wise. There was one class and activity that did cross my mind, debate. I was on the debate team. You want to know what it feels like to have an adrenaline filled high while not doing any physical activity? Try debate. It is filled with loads and loads of research and cited articles (and sometimes only one line from a certain article) that you cram into your brain for a verbal jousting match amongst your teenage peers. I didn't win every match and never made it to the highest-level squad of my school's team, but participating on the debate team pushed me into places mentally and emotionally that I never thought possible. The mental toughness that debate engrained in me turned out to be an invaluable skill that I still use today.

So here was the big question for me: how do I turn debate into a major and then a career? Law school didn't interest me. It seemed too tedious and would require several more years of school after my undergrad. I literally (as a soon-to-be sophomore at the University of Kansas) got out the course catalog and started reading. I found that a journalism major,

*Introduction*

with an emphasis in strategic communications seemed to fit what I was after.

I promptly switched majors and enrolled in a new slate of classes for the fall. I know that everyone has had their own unique post-high school and college experiences. Mine did not follow the typical four or even five-year plan for a higher education degree. I am proud to say that I am a graduate of the University of Kansas with a Bachelor of Arts degree earned after seven years of hard work, detours, debt, parking myself outside of the door of many admissions directors, and asking lots and lots of questions. I make no joke about this: college is HARD, not just the course work but navigating the higher education system. Tuition is expensive. You have to want a college degree bad enough to go through all hoops placed in front of you to get the degree. For me, it was applying for in-state tuition after several years of paying state income taxes, making Kansas my permanent residence, registering to vote, joining a church, and even helping to campaign for a gubernatorial candidate. I persevered because I felt that a college degree would at least give me the marketable credentials needed in the job market to be able to start a career.

While working at JC Penney during my junior year, the local newspaper's advertising director walked in with their photographer to take photos for an upcoming ad. They looked like they were having fun, and this seemed like something I'd like to be a part of. I went out on a limb and asked if they were hiring summer interns. The advertising director said to stop by and apply; and the next day, I did just that.

That interaction took guts. I took advantage of a situation that I had not planned or prepared for. I was shocked that I was even hired. I worked as an advertising intern for that newspaper for the summer and grew it into a full-time job as an advertising executive. This all happened before I ever graduated from college.

As a barely twenty-something nobody, I was intimidated by my superiors, more seasoned colleagues, and the clients I was asked to recruit. I decided that the best way to learn something was to jump into the deep end and take on the difficult clients. That meant doing the jobs that no one wanted to do. As I worked my way up, in addition to my positions in sales, I hauled boxes, set up tables and chairs, served (and cooked) food, cleaned up after events, and worked to make my company's brand shine. There was not a single college class that could have prepared me for this side of business.

Many of the events I was asked to participate in for work were charity golf events. I was never asked to actually play (and in fact my male bosses never asked me if I could play) but was told to make our presence at the hole, or after party, look amazing. Year after year, as many of the same people (and these were the movers and shakers of the community) forgot my name as they grabbed a free koozie or other giveaway item, I realized something: most of the players who were attending these charity golf events were men, and they were doing business as they golfed. They were not schlepping heavy boxes of giveaways. They were not setting up tents and tables and chairs in crappy weather. They were cruising on by with smiles on their faces, the benefactors of what I was providing.

I decided something had to change. I needed to figure out how I could get on the other side of that situation by being the golfer. As I thought more about it, I realized that being the golfer on the course was one thing but using activities like golf to network and get deals done was the end goal. It occurred to me that I was afraid. Was I afraid of embarrassing myself in front of good golfers? Was it a fear of even trying? And even more importantly, why does is HAVE to be golf? Why can't there be other activities that are just as impactful as golf that women can participate in to have the same results?

This book is my explanation of how to embrace your fear of something that you quite frankly, suck at. For many of you reading this book, golf may be the number one thing you do poorly. This book is the start and continuation of a conversation about how male golfers use golf as a means to an end (whether the end be purely social or the closing of big deals with clients). It is about changing your perception of what is a socially acceptable way to do things and taking charge of who you are and where you want to be.

*Golfing In Heels* is my story about getting out of your own way and trying something new. It is my hope that you take the elements in this book and find a way to apply them to any part of your life that you seek to improve. As a working mom and wife, I have been challenged to juggle home and work life and feel like I am actually accomplishing something. We as women do a lot, and I want to share with you ways to make it easier. Your value shouldn't be measured by how many times you whiff and miss, but how you showed up and asked for more.

I hope you get to experience a bit of my humor, life lessons, and words of encouragement. We all have our own stories to tell. I hope you enjoy mine, even while doing it in heels!

**CHAPTER 1**

# *Golf is Not Just a Man's Game*

**MY DAD GOLFS,** so does my brother, husband, boss, and most of the men I know. If you ask a guy why they golf, most will answer that it is relaxing, fun, and an enjoyable activity to do with friends. I think men are onto something here. How many women do you know who participate regularly in activities that take the better part of a day, are encouraged by their employers, may lead to new opportunities, provide socialization, are conducted in (mostly) beautiful weather, and are exercise? None come to the top of my mind.

Ladies—we need to take advantage of an activity that our male counterparts have known about for years.

# GOLFING IN HEELS

> *My boss phoned me today. He said, "Is everything okay at the office?"*
> *I said, "Yes, it's all under control. It's been a very busy day, I haven't stopped."*
> *"Can you do me a favor?" he asked.*
> *I said "Of course, what is it?"*
> *"Speed up a little. I'm the foursome behind you."*
> Anonymous

Men have dominated the sports profession since the beginning of time. If your weekends look anything like mine, then you are notified of the seasons changing not by the weather, but by what sport is playing on television. From the crowd roaring football games, to the buzzing of race cars zooming around the track, the seasons merge right into each other. I do know a few ladies who enjoy a good sporting event, but they do not plan their work, travel, and leisure schedules around them.

Sports, for men, are competitive, fun, and engaging activities that they pursue in those pockets of time in and around their workday. They seek out sport as a way to connect with others and to provide their input to generate affiliation. Even if there is disagreement in the board room, many times there is total agreement on the course, court, or ball field. Participation in sports creates an atmosphere of inclusion that will many times override the push of a sales pitch to get deals done.

### Why Women Should Get into the Game

We hurry everywhere. We hurry to get the kids off to school, we hurry to work, and we hurry home to make dinner. When you do find that unexpected moment of calm, do you know what to do with yourself? Do you ever plan for some down time?

What are some things you hurry to? Is it getting out the door in the morning? Is it getting a meal prepared, or getting your errands completed? Take a minute to write down the areas where you feel hurried.

_____

_____

_____

_____

_____

_____

_____

As you look at the list you just made above, I hope you give yourself a big pat on the back for being superwoman (because you are!) and also for all that you are accomplishing in a day or in a week's time. Being hurried makes us less productive and takes away from our ability to be good at any one thing, not to mention making us stressed out! I hear my own self talk repeating, "if I only had more time." Here is the reality: even though there are only 24 hours in a day, we have a choice about how we spend them. Let me say that again. We have a **choice** about how we spend time.

> *"You're only here for a short visit. Don't hurry. Don't worry. And, be sure to smell the flowers along the way."* —Walter Hagen

Making choices about how we spend our time takes some guts. We, as women, tend to ride the guilt train like there is no tomorrow. We ask ourselves "What if this (insert task) doesn't get done?" Well, what if it doesn't get done? What are the consequences of those actions? The more important question is who can you ask for help to get everything done?

Identifying those people in our lives who can be helpers (and that includes our kids too) creates space to make the ask for help. Who are those people in your life that you can ask to help? These people may only be good at certain tasks, but I want you to write them down anyway.

_____

_____

_____

_____

_____

My goal in getting you thinking about an activity like golf in the space of your crazy lives is to retrain your brain into considering new areas of growth. If the idea of picking up a golf club for the first time or even thinking about how you can possibly squeeze in time for trying out this game seems way out of your comfort zone, take it a little slower. What if you could open up minutes of your day to breathe a little deeper, to find white space in your mind and spirit?

I am going to share a full disclosure comment here: I don't expect you to love golf. I don't even expect you to like golf. I want to challenge you to think about the game of golf in a way that gets you thinking outside of your everyday. You may find that my ideas in this book apply to a completely different activity, and that is ok. We, amazing women of the world, are here to create powerful moments for ourselves and the people we interact with to produce meaningful and productive outcomes. If you learn anything from this book, I hope you take the nuggets of golf wisdom and apply them to any and all parts of your life.

The game of golf was not created to be a form of stress relief. In fact, many professional golfers feel that the game is actually stressful — especially when they are playing to win. While healthy competition can be positive, adding a level of stress to something so enjoyable cannot be good for you. To get started in any new skill, you need to carry along an open mind and lot of humor.

There have been time lapses of years when I haven't picked up a golf club. I would not say that returning to the sport is just like riding a bike, but the basics do come back pretty quickly. For me, taking a swing for the first time in a long while is a lot like slipping into your favorite outfit — it feels good, powerful, and effortless. That "ching" as your club strikes the ball seals the deal to complete your experience.

I want you to take a minute and write down:

1) Why do you currently play golf (if you are currently a player)?

_____

_____

_____

_____


2) Why are you considering trying out golf?

_____

_____

_____

_____


3) What are your fears about learning the game of golf?

_____

_____

Raise your hand if you've never picked up a club in your life? I have met many women who are scared to death to pick up a club and have never set foot on a course. It could be that no one has ever asked them to play, or many times, it is just an unknown activity for them. What is stopping you? Is it cost, lack of interest, your non-athletic ability, fear of looking like a fool? I am going to remove all of those boundaries for you right now.

If cost is an issue: find a friend or family member who golfs and ask to borrow their clubs. I guarantee you that they will even have a few old irons or woods around to pass off to you for free. The fit of their clubs may not be ideal, but the object here is not to make you perfect, it is just to get you started. If you don't know anyone who golfs, or who is willing to loan you some clubs, then you can rent them at most courses and driving ranges. Golf club rental is a great way to test out a variety of clubs for a fraction of the cost of a new set.

According to a golfweek.com survey in December of 2018, the average price of a round of golf (that is 18 holes) is $36 at a public course including cart rental. If you need to rent a set of clubs as well, public course pricing for club rental can start as low as $15 according to wheresmycaddie.com. It is more affordable than you think.

Instead of starting on the course, a less intimidating way may be to start at the driving range. There are many available public, private, and even indoor driving range options that make golf even more affordable. And better yet, practicing golf at a driving range requires a time commitment that is customized to your schedule (whether it be 10 minutes or an entire afternoon).

My first set of golf clubs was a hodgepodge of old clubs from my parents. I even had some real wood drivers that are probably now worth something if I tried to sell them. I was not a pretty sight at the golf course, but I was getting out there.

*The Benefits of Playing Golf*

Try this on for size. At the end of a long stressful day, one of the ways I like to let off a little steam is to do a physical activity. The adrenalin rush not only forces endorphins into my brain for that feel-good response, but it also gets out the frustrations of the day. There is something so gratifying about using your physical strength to move a tiny object a long distance at remarkable speed.

The slower pace of golf creates an opportunity for people of all physical shapes and sizes to participate. This activity is not only for the physically elite and does not discriminate based on age, either. Golf is an activity that can be started at any time in life.

Take a friend with you. The slower pace of golf allows for some good social interaction. A date at the driving range is of minimal cost, and maximum impact. You will spend less renting a bucket of balls than you would spend going out to eat. Doing something outside of your normal day-to-day activities with a social element is the perfect combination for decompression.

Are you excited to give golf a try now? What opportunities can you incorporate into golf? Is it a socializing time, exercise, or a way to destress? Write your ideas below.

_____

_____

_____

_____

_____

*"You can't call it a sport. You don't run, jump, you don't shoot, you don't pass. All you have to do is buy some clothes that don't match."* —Steve Sax

I always have a hard time convincing the not-so-athletic ladies to pick up a club. Here is a little secret about golf: it doesn't matter what shape you are, how tall you are, and if you have an ounce of coordination or physical strength. The beauty of golf is that it does not discriminate.

Can't walk 18-holes? No problem! There are cute little golf carts to get you from hole to hole. I would suggest starting on a nine-hole course (or just playing nine holes on an eighteen-hole course). That way, your time commitment is less, and you can walk the course if you choose. Growing up, I had this nine-hole course close to my house. Because it was only nine holes, carts were not an option. It was also an easy course, with every hole being a par 3 or 4. It was a great place to get started with the game.

I'm just going to get this out of the way right now: I have looked like a fool playing golf. I have swung and missed, hit myself with my own ball, and fell over from the momentum of trying too hard. Even the pros have flubbed up and missed the ball, landed one in the water, hit a tree, hit a person — You name it, and it has been done. I want to give you the confidence to not only try golf, but to have a great sense of humor when trying.

I played in a golf tournament recently with my husband and some good friends. On the last hole, we decided to have a little fun. We recorded each other taking "Happy Gilmore" shots at the tee box. If you haven't seen Adam Sandler play golf in the movie "Happy Gilmore," then here's a description of the shot. In "Happy Gilmore," the golf club of choice is a hockey stick. The face of a hockey stick is clearly bigger than a golf club and affords "Happy" with an advantage over his competition. The problem is, "Happy" is not a golfer. He is a hockey player. When he sets up his drive on the golf course, he takes a running start before making contact with the ball.

We all took heed from "Happy" and lined up and took a running start towards our ball at the tee box. Needless to say, I missed the ball. I missed it three times. This experience was all recorded on my husband's smart phone and posted on Facebook for the world to see. The best part about this experience for me was laughing hysterically the entire time. I still get the giggles just thinking about it.

> *"The reason the pro tells you to keep your head down is so you can't see him laughing"* —Phyllis Diller

Golf is a slow game to play. This used to bother me — a lot. Being a Type-A personality, I needed to go fast and faster everywhere. Who has time to play golf anyway? I can think of all the things I would rather do with 5 hours of my day. I can, even more importantly, think of all the things I need to cross off my to-do list in that amount of time.

Evaluating and valuing your time is a fairly new concept for me. If you asked me a couple of years ago how much of a value my free time was to me, I would have said "priceless," and then followed it up with "what free time?" These are quite opposite ends of the spectrum. Either my time was worth more than all the money in the world, or it wasn't worth anything because there was none to be had. There had to be a happy medium to this equation.

My friend and Executive Coach, Jay Pryor, asked me a riveting question about my time. They asked me "how much do you make an hour?" I thought of that figure in my head (and I want you to think of that figure, too) and then they followed up with "would you pay someone your wage per hour to do \_\_\_\_?" This made me really evaluate the time I spend doing those "have to" things like cleaning, laundry, multiple errands and more. If I had to pay myself a wage to do these things, would I continue to do them, or would I hire them out?

I made a bold decision and hired a cleaning person for the first time. It was bold for me, because that neurotic personality I have kept telling myself that I didn't need to hire out house cleaning, and that I could do it better and more efficiently than anyone else. It came to a head one Saturday, when my daughter asked me five times in the course of an hour to read a book with her. I was scrubbing the bathroom at this time and kept repeating the phrase "just a minute!" That minute turned into four hours. I honestly did not think it took me four hours to clean my house. I could rationalize this time because I was "multi-tasking" and actually getting many things done throughout the course of those four hours. Yeah right!

Since I made the decision to outsource a little bit of my "to do" list each week, the time I now have is "priceless" and growing in quantity. The time I have gained, has allowed me to take deep breaths, snuggle with the kiddos on Saturday mornings, and low and behold — work in a little golf.

Thinking about how you can outsource your "to do" list doesn't have to mean spending money. I know that some of the skills that my family and friends have differ from my own, and a way to take advantage of your strengths and time is to barter them for maximum benefit. Perhaps it is meal preparation. If you have a friend who loves to cook, offer to watch her children for a few hours in exchange for some crockpot ready meals put together for you for the week. You can buy the groceries, and she can assemble them for you.

You can also incorporate those "to do" list items into a social event. Tackle those projects with a friend, and use the time spent together to catch up on each other's lives.

What are some time management solutions you can incorporate into your life?

_____

_____

_____

_____

_____

*Think Like the Guys*

Ask most men what their plans are for the weekend, and I guarantee their answers have nothing to do with housework, errands or kid stuff. Not to say that those "have to" activities won't happen for them, but the first thing out of their mouths is something fun and relaxing. Think of this for a moment. What if the first idea about how you are going to spend your down time is something you enjoy? Could you set aside the laundry list of things that are clogging up your brain temporarily to relish on the "get to" instead of on the "have to?"

Take a minute to write down all the things you want to get crossed off your "to do" list:

Women tend to deprioritize their own needs. In a Huffington Post article titled "Why Do Women Find it so Difficult to Put Themselves First?" author Rosjke Hasseldine calls out "The Culture of Female Service." She explains that "(t)his is an umbrella term I use to cover all the cultural beliefs that we have about how females are the nurturing gender, and that it is a woman's role and duty to care-for and nurture their family and community, without needing care in return." Whether you are a mother, boss, wife, sister, or a good friend, we females need to speak up. I am a huge personal de-prioritizer. I am at fault for making the mental list, then the grocery list, then the to-do list for all the "have to's" each and every day. Those items creep up into my conscious before my eyes are open in the morning. I have even woken up from a deep sleep because I was afraid I forgot to check off one of those items on my list. This requires much more than a simple lesson on "focusing on the positive." It requires a re-training of how you think about your time.

Growing up, my family liked to take vacations each summer where we would travel cross-country in the car. Being gone for weeks at a time, we had to pack accordingly. My parents gave each of us kids one suitcase to take, and all our clothes, shoes, and whatever else we insisted on bringing with us had to fit in that one suitcase. I would make lists of the outfits I planned to bring, matching the tops to the bottoms, coordinating shoes and accessories. I would start packing days or even a week in advance. My suitcase was stuffed to the gills. When we would return home, I was amazed to discover that I did not wear everything in my suitcase. After all of that careful planning and list making, I chose the outfits that I liked the best and forgot about the rest.

While I was unpacking from these trips, I thought to myself "next time, I'm not taking this much." But when the next trip would come along, fear would set in. What if I didn't have that right outfit for that right event? What if I couldn't launder the clothes that I liked to wear and was stuck in something uncoordinated? Or <gasp!> what if I had to wear something two days in a row? I am laughing at this behavior now, but back then, it was my complete reality.

Do you think men think like this? I have no doubt that the guys are prepared, but when it comes right down to it, they can get creative and make something work.

How could you "think like the guys" in your life? What would you do differently?

_____

_____

_____

_____

_____

_____

*Delegate, Delegate, and Delegate Some More*

Most of the women I know are "doers." They multitask, scale buildings in a single bound, whip up dinner while curling their hair — you get the picture. I was at a party recently with some wonderful, driven, and successful women when the discussion turned to the all too familiar dynamic of men vs. women. Each woman at the party was in a serious relationship (either married or dating) and had much to offer up on this topic. As I listened to these ladies describe their trials and tribulations with their mates, I understood that the same conclusion could be drawn amongst us all. We, as women, do not ask for help easily.

Author Nina Manolson describes in her blog post "The Top 3 Reasons Women Don't Ask for Help and How to

Bypass Them" why we have such a hard time with this issue. She shares her top three as:

I KNOW
*"I already know **what** to do and what to eat, to feel good…I should just do it myself! I shouldn't have to ask for help."*

FAILURE
*"I've tried so many things before, to feel good in my body, and if I ask for help, I'm going to fail again…"*

TRUST
*"I don't know if anyone can really help me. I'm really unique…"*

*Do these examples sound like you? What are your reasons for not asking for help?*

_____

_____

_____

_____

_____

One woman described a typical evening at her house. As a full-time working mother of two, both she and her husband arrive home each night to a routine of dinner, schoolwork, bath time, and stories before bed. "It never fails," she said, "that my husband gets in the door and plops himself in front of the computer or the TV, while I'm running around trying to get dinner on the table." She went on to share, with the rest of us nodding in agreement, that "he doesn't even offer to help!"

After dishing about our frustrations, then giving them a good laugh, we came to a conclusion. When asked, our guys are more than happy to pitch in. The problem is we women don't think we should have to ask. We assume that our men will see our flurry of activity and jump up to help. It isn't until our stress level is about to burst through the roof that we scream out "can I get some help here please?!" Boy, doesn't that make you want to hop up and help that formerly charming, beautiful, and loving woman whom you have shared your heart with now that she has sprouted horns and breathes fire?

What do you need help with that you are afraid to ask?

_____

_____

_____

_____

_____

Let's take a step back for a minute and take a hint from our male counterparts. What if you came home and plopped yourself down in front of the TV and zoned out the rest of the world as soon as you got home. How would you feel? I bet guilty is the first feeling that comes to mind, and the next feeling would be your children and/or significant other whining in your ear about how hungry they are. You could temporarily relieve these feelings by purchasing a good pair of earphones, eye mask, and concrete room that is bolted with a steel lock. There, that ought to keep them away. But eventually, they would pick the lock, rip off your eye mask, and turn off the calming music you had playing through your earphones, and you are back to square one. What does this prove? You are the action that creates the reaction.

*"Give me the fresh air, a beautiful partner, and a nice round of golf, and you can keep the fresh air and the round of golf." —Jack Benny*

We must learn to effectively delegate. As my own children get older, I am happily enjoying the benefits of their physical capacity to do some housework. My kids are capable of picking up their rooms, setting and clearing the table, getting themselves ready in the morning and at bedtime, and more! It has not only been a load off my shoulders, but a growing experience in responsibility for them as well. The expectation of our household is for them to pitch in.

So why is it so hard for women to ask for help from the men? Men do it all the time, and they usually ask us in a sweet, endearing voice that makes us always say "yes." Hmmmm. I think they are onto something here. Asking nicely, using a calm voice, and getting what we want can be achieved a lot more easily than you think. It will definitely take some practice because this will be a new action for many of us.

What about other aspects of your life? Do you ask for help when you need it? Think about what tasks you can get off your plate and delegate to someone who could use them as a learning experience, or who has the capacity to get them done better and faster.

What tasks can you delegate to others right now?

_____

_____

_____

_____

_____

For years, I assisted one of my colleagues with a weekly task of typing up and printing off a certain report. This report didn't directly affect my job but was beneficial to our organization as a whole. I was asked to take on this task as a favor, and being the can-do person I am, I immediately accepted. As time went on, the time that I was able to allocate to completing these reports was diminished due to increasing responsibilities within my own position. I finally summoned up the nerve to delegate this task away from myself and suggested that a newer staff member take on this responsibility. That new staff member was overjoyed to be asked to take on a new task and proceeded with gusto. In addition to just completing the reports as asked, this staffer came up with a creative way to enhance the reports all together. This became a true win-win situation, removing something menial off of my plate and creating a learning opportunity to do something greater for another.

When your path is clear, think of all the things you can do. Take a look at the list of items you just wrote down that could be delegated and shift your focus to the things you could now accomplish with that free time and space. What are you capable of doing now if those items are off your plate?

_____

_____

_____

_____

_____

_____

_____

## GOLFING IN HEELS

I successfully cajoled several of my best gal pals into golfing with me. I started in on them early, with a plea to support charity, enjoy some fresh air, and the promise of Wi-Fi access on the course. Being the "go-for-it" women I know them for, they all agreed to sign up and pay their greens fees. There, now I had them! A few days before the golf event, I received a nervous email from one of my gals. She was an inexperienced golfer and did not want to look ridiculous playing golf in a rather large tournament where she would know other people (especially those men). I assured her, that only us girls would be around to see her take a swing, and if she messed up, we were there to laugh right along with her.

We set off together with our coolers full of lite beer (and some remarkably cute gift bags I put together for them) and hit the links. That first tee was daunting, but we all made contact with the ball. I was so proud of my friends for getting way outside of their comfort zones and embarking on this adventure with me for the day.

List some times when you had to step outside of your comfort zone and ended up having a blast!

We ended up playing sixteen out of the eighteen holes, due to a friendly golf marshal who suggested that we "pick up the pace" a bit to keep the other golfers on track. We were relieved to skip ahead and put more distance between ourselves the other golfers. Now the fun could really begin. Downing another lite beer, we got into our groove. This event was a scramble format (which means that instead of every player being responsible for individual strokes on each hole, you play as a team and take advantage of the best players ball placement and move your ball to their position) and I am happy to say that we used every player's ball at least once. Our foursome found our strengths through our drives, putts, and silly sense of humor. We finished the tournament way over par, but with smiles on our faces. The day proved to be a success. We learned new skills, tried new moves, and most of all enjoyed some much-needed stress-free time.

# CHAPTER 2

# *I am Not a Golfer*

*"Golf and sex are the only things you can enjoy without being good at them"* —*Jimmy DeMaret*

**I STRUGGLE WITH** trying new things that do not appear to be fun to me. In fact, I can create a good long list of things that I am "not" in my life. Let's get started with you and identify those things in your life that you struggle with and list them out below:

_____

_____

_____

_____

_____

My mother loves to garden. The second she arrives home each day, she immediately goes inside to change her clothes so she can dig in the dirt. She creates masterpieces out of nothing and has beautiful flowers and plants to show for it. She spends more time weeding and planting than she does cleaning her house. I have always been amazed at her passion and enjoyment for something that I don't see as fun. Why would I want to relax by getting dirty and pulling weeds? She is constantly after me to replant this or move that plant to another location in my yard where it will thrive better. I recognize that she is telling me all of this in love, but one thing rings true: I am not a gardener. I enjoy looking at gardens, but the thought of getting down and dirty in them is another story.

What I admire most about my mom and her love of gardening, is her passion for recognizing a skill that produces an outcome that I also want to achieve. I have pushed back on gardening over the years because I shut down at the beginning of the activity. I've shared with you that getting dirty and pulling weeds doesn't seem relaxing to me. In fact, it appears like work. What if I shifted my perspective of this one activity and instead focused on the outcome of producing beautiful things to look at? Would that help change my attitude and encourage me to give it more of a try?

## I am Not a Golfer

As a child, my Dad took me out to play golf. I was probably eleven or twelve at the time. One of his passions is teaching, and with it he enjoyed teaching me the game of golf. Every stroke, every club, every hole he lined me up, positioned my hands, and talked me through the perfect swing. The best part about those experiences was when we would walk together between shots. His intentions were good, but my mind was definitely not on golf. I didn't care what the "correct" way to hold a club was, or how I needed to align my feet. I just wanted to hit the ball and be done with it.

Years later, I was asked to play in a golf tournament on behalf of my company. I "played" golf, but definitely didn't enjoy it. We had one spot left to fill on the team, so I asked my husband to join us. My husband is one of those natural athletes who can pick up a sport and play fairly well in a short amount of time. So, needless to say, he was playing to show his skills and carried our team for much of the tournament. As the hours dragged on, I found myself noticing how he was so relaxed. He was playing well. He was smiling. He was complimenting me (even though I played poorly), and the time we spent together was priceless. We had such a great time together that day. I do not remember what the score was, or how many balls I lost, but I definitely remembered the fun we had.

At the end of the day, I was sweaty, smelly, and very happy. I realized that day that I am definitely not a golfer and that golf is a struggle for me but I discovered that I do enjoy the golf experience. I tried to think of another time that I was able to spend 5 hours with my husband (sans kids) and not feel guilty about it. My mind was relaxed. I noticed the beautiful landscaping of the course and took in lots of fresh air. It was good for my soul to be out there that day.

When was the last time you let go of your struggle and dislike for an activity, and let yourself enjoy the moment?

_____

_____

_____

_____

_____

_____

So often we set ourselves up for failure before we even begin. We anticipate everything that can go wrong and imagine how we are going to feel about the activity. We give our brains a "worst case scenario" outcome. Here is the truth behind this kind of thinking:

You, and you alone, will create the feeling (good or bad) that will ultimately determine how much you enjoy the activity well before you get started. You can talk yourself into or out of just about any feeling.

I want you to take a minute and shift this perspective. If you agree that our thoughts produce feelings even before we are in the thick of the experience itself, think about how you can shift your thought process to create good feelings. What if you gave yourself a bit of a pep talk before a seemingly daunting experience to focus on the best-case scenario?

> *"When I die, bury me on the golf course so my husband will visit"* —Author Unknown

This exercise starts with identifying your strengths and how they can impact your attitude. Use the space below to jot down your strengths as they relate to your struggles. I'll help get you started:

Struggle: Enjoying time with my family when there is a pile of laundry to be done.

Strength: I can ask my family to help me tackle the laundry so we can all enjoy time together.

_____

_____

_____

_____

_____

_____

_____

_____

Identifying your strengths can be a bit of a challenge. I had a conversation recently with some female friends about the challenge that plagues many women today, planning and making dinner every night. One of the ladies piped up with a simple antidote for our weakness. She admitted that she, like me, didn't enjoy cooking. Her challenge was that he didn't like to plan or shop for the food, only to prepare the meal. Her solution? She did the meal planning a month in advance and coordinated all the ingredient shopping. Her husband was left with what he liked to do: cooking great tasting and healthy meals for their family. I asked her how she made this arrangement work, and her response was that she did what she liked to do best (coordinating and clean-up) and let her husband do what he liked to do best (cooking).

I am a huge advocate for removing the words "I can't" from a person's vocabulary. Now, it may be the case that because of my height, I can't reach something on the top shelf, but I sure can figure out a way to get that item down — say with a step stool. I remember making my father-in-law gasp a few times when I ran up and down step stools to reach high objects while very pregnant with each of my two kids. Not that everyone should try this task, but there are always solutions to everything.

On my quest to discover why I and others are not golfers, I have been amused by the responses I have received. Most women respond to me with a deer in the headlights look and stammer out their answer with something like, "oh, I don't do that sort of thing." When I follow this up with "what sort of thing?" I get a "you know, that golf sort of thing."

So, what in the world is this "golf sort of thing?" I'll tell you. It is not some big secret. It is not scary. It won't hurt. It is not bad for you, and if you give it a try, you may want to come back for more.

Women have the tendency to tell you everything they are not. What I've witnessed is that women are stronger than steel, have the endurance of a tri-athlete, and the perseverance to stick it out until it's done right. They will kick-ass and then melt softly into the background so others can take the glory.

Self-help guru Tony Robbins says that "fear and courage are physical." He encourages you to experience this phenomenon by creating a physical action that makes you feel powerful. I want you to try something with me right now. I want you to stand up, shout "YEAH!" and pump your fist. If you are somewhere where this expression is not possible, then head to YouTube and watch a video of someone doing this same action.

What physical action can you do that gives you a sense of power?

_____

_____

_____

_____

I took my son to a new children's exhibit recently. He was immediately lured over to an area where kids could put together building block versions of race cars and speed them down a track. The two of us put together something that sort-of resembled a car: it had wheels and a middle part to hold it all together. He grabbed it out of my hand and headed for the track, ignoring my protests of "we need to add more to it." He didn't care. He wanted to see it go, and go it did. When his car made it to the end of the track, he was all fist-pumps, and "whoo hoo's" and "YEEEAAAAHHH!" Just watching him experience this elation put a big smile on my face. I wanted to jump up and down with him and share in his joy. I opted instead for lots of high-fives, and "way to go's." I was amazed that a thrown together toy car could have such a profound impact on him. You would have thought that I had given him a shiny new car with all the bells and whistles.

The simple actions that my son experienced and showed me that day were magical. I watched other parents and children put together intricate vehicles that would have made an engineer proud. But during the time that they were making their cars, my little boy was bubbling over with excitement. He knew what mattered most to him: getting to celebrate his simple creation.

Empowerment is a trait that we all can experience. It doesn't have to take the form of something big. A few years ago, I was headed into work when one of my tires went flat. Fortunately, I was near a gas station, and pulled in to take a look. The gas station didn't have any services (only gas and a small convenience store) so there wasn't anyone there to assist. I did have a roadside assistance plan but decided that if I took a look at my owner's manual, I might be able to figure out how to change a tire.

A few minutes later, this nice older gentleman pulled up and asked if I needed help. "No thank you." I told him. He smiled, and shared that he had a daughter about my age, and she was perfectly capable of changing her own tire, too. He stopped in at the convenience store for a cup of coffee, and on his way out said that he would hang out for a bit just in case I had any questions. Truth be told: I did have some questions. He graciously suggested that I loosen the lug nuts slightly before I jacked up the car. He then gave me some space while I finished changing the tire all by myself. That day of changing a tire in work clothes was amazing. I felt like I could do anything! Since that day, I have successfully changed every tire on that car and more. We have the ability to do more than we think we are capable of. We have resources within us that we only need to tap into to unleash our full abilities. And for me, in this case, I knew how to locate and read my car's owner's manual.

*Celebrate Even the Smallest Things*

What can you celebrate right now? Even if it is the smallest thing like the sun shining, receiving a smile from a stranger, or getting out the door on time, celebrate it and write it down below.

## GOLFING IN HEELS

I am a list maker. I make grocery lists, to-do lists, bucket lists, and on and on. A huge sense of fulfillment comes over me when I cross the last item on that list off. The satisfaction almost gives me permission to turn over a fresh page and start anew. But wait a minute. I just spent a large amount of time and energy knocking out all those items on my list. Don't I even get a pat on the back or something?

Turning small successes into motivation for bigger things takes practice. Just like any habit, repetition over time creates bigger change. By starting small, you are creating the building blocks that will move you to the next level. If you take these elements and apply them to the golf course (like taking the same swing over and over again, or even just showing up to the golf course or driving range), the small steps will eventually become easier.

Momentum can be your best ally or your biggest enemy. Once you get started with something (i.e. tackling that to-do list), it is easier to keep going. The challenge is getting up the motivation to get started. One of my least favorite household chores is doing the laundry. Correct that — my least favorite household chore is *folding and putting away* clean laundry. This has to be the most boring and time-consuming activity around. If it weren't for the fact that I like to wear clean clothes, I would probably put it off more than I do. My motivation for getting the laundry done is (and I hate to say it) television. Most of the housework in our home is done on the weekends. My husband and I are usually up before the kids are. I use this quiet time to start a pot of coffee and then scoop the dirty laundry, towels, sheets, and everything else into the laundry room and start the washing machine. While the first load washes, I settle in for some TV surfing time. I use the commercial breaks to switch the completed wash load into the dryer or for folding a load from the dryer. Now that's motivation! Commercial breaks are only a couple of minutes long. I have found that the white loads (the ones with all of the socks and underwear) pose the biggest time crunch for folding during commercial breaks, but it can be done.

As a reward for my domestic goddess abilities: I get a few minutes of snuggle time on the couch with either my hubby or my kiddos while sipping my coveted morning brew. This also frees me up later in the day for some book and magazine reading time or perhaps a trip to the store for some yummy refreshments to celebrate with at dinner. By carving out the time to reward yourself for hard work, you are incentivizing your ego to keep it up.

"I am not a golfer" encompasses more than just golf. The "I am not" part of life is a challenge, and I'll admit it…I am not a lot of things.

Ann Herold, author of "Uh, Listen, Ma'am, May I make a Suggestion?" printed in *FORE* magazine's May/June 2012 issue expressed her views beautifully on why women are not golfers. Herold writes "(w)omen generally enter the world of golf with three strikes against them. Boys get taken to the course by their dads, granddads, uncles, and family friends as children. Girls don't. Though they should. There's nothing like the swing developed in youth, when the mind seizes the muscle memory and makes it unconscious, like breathing."

If you think about the activities you were engaged in growing up, did any of them include golf? I am probably an anomaly, but even with my early introduction to the game of golf, I still don't consider myself in the golfer category. What I want to know is: why aren't we taking out our daughters, granddaughters, nieces, and little sisters out to the course? Golf is definitely not a contact sport (well, that is if you don't hit anyone with your wayward ball) and doesn't require padding, a helmet, or special shoes (for the most part). I don't even consider the game to be even all that masculine. Sure, it is a sport, and the more athletic you are, the greater your potential is for fine tuning your strokes, distance, and more. There also is nothing in the rule book that recommends an appropriate age to begin, or for that matter, an age to stop.

Tiger Woods' father had him hitting golf balls as a toddler. If you watch his swing, you will see the ease and perfection that he has mastered from being exposed to golf at an early age. My kids have the kid's plastic variety golf play set and enjoy whacking a ball or other object around for fun. We have recently begun to show my daughter the proper way to hold a real club and how to swing. I am excited to get her involved in the game and see where she takes it. Golf, for her, may be just something that she understands, but maybe won't enjoy and pursue. On the other hand, golf may prove to open doors for her as she gets older.

I was introduced to a college golf coach at a charity golf event a few years ago. In asking her where her players were from, I was surprised that they were from all over the world. She shared that they were having a hard time finding female college athletes that play golf closer to home, even with the scholarship potential available to them. Wait... what?!?! There are college scholarships available, but there are not enough females playing golf to fill the slots on the college team? This not only surprised me, but disappointed me. There is an opportunity here for even younger girls to get into the game. Now, not every college or university has a women's golf team, nor has scholarships available for golf, but the fact that this seasoned coach could not even find players to evaluate was dumbfounding to me.

Ladies, golf is a lifelong sport available to everyone. As I shared earlier, it doesn't take a certain body type to play. There are opportunities, from a free college education to networking opportunities with your superiors and potential clients, that exist on the golf course. I'm not saying this is the only way to succeed, but it is one area that women are not engaging in that can provide a platform for success.

*Getting Started*

New ventures take a little bit of luck and a lot of what the heck! Trying new things makes your heart beat a little faster and your mouth get dry; and sometimes, a little light headedness and nausea is thrown in. This would be yours truly on a roller coaster. I think all of us are adrenalin junkies — at least a little bit. Adrenalin creates that fight-or-flight response in our bodies that revs up every muscle and organ to its maximum. On the roller coaster, my adrenalin starts to rise as I'm climbing the first incline where the angle of the drop on the other side will make my stomach leave my body momentarily. Although I have had the huge urge to tell them to stop the ride and let me off (flight response), I know that I will be ok, and that such requests are really only for serious emergencies.

Instead, I whip into fight mode. I cling onto the safety bar for dear life and scream my head off as we go catapulting down the incline at what seems like 100 mph. As we rush up the other side, my adrenaline high leaves me with the giggles and I am all in. The intensity of a roller coaster ride may not be for everyone but experiencing the peak of your body's ability to cope with something extreme is remarkable.

How to you get started with a new activity? I used the adrenalin example to create a memory in my brain of something exhilarating. Remembering the thrill after riding that roller coaster (or other activity that you maybe didn't want to do at first) creates the power to get up the nerve to do something else.

Take a minute to write down below what motivates you to take that first step.

_____

_____

_____

_____

_____

My daughter is reaching an age where she can do more and more things by herself. I tested her out one day when we were out to lunch. As we were finishing our meal, my daughter asked if she could have dessert. Since she did a great job with lunch that day, I said "sure." But here was the caveat: she had to go up to the counter and order and pay for the dessert herself. Her eyes got wide, and she stammered out a protest. I handed her the money and told her I would be right here at the table waiting for her (a mere 10 feet away). She had to decide what she wanted more: the dessert, or the anticlimactic decision of staying put. I knew she really wanted that dessert (who wouldn't?), and she had a tough decision to make.

She took a deep breath and looked over at the counter of the restaurant. She inched her way out of the booth and walked slowly to the register. I could barely hear her say the words to the guy behind the counter, but he smiled at her and helped her select a chocolate brownie from the glass case in front. She gave him the bill for payment, and he gave her change back. She said, "thank you," and headed back to the table with a huge smile on her face.

I know that the new experience factor was off the charts for her that day, but it was also off the charts for me as well. As a parent, I had always taken care of things for her. It was a test of both of our comfort levels to engage in a new activity, even something as simple as ordering dessert. We both learned new skills and gained an appreciation for trusting our own personal abilities.

For me, I took the leap a number of years ago and decided to put a team together for a charity golf event. I had normally volunteered to set up a table on a hole with our company's sponsorship information to hand out. My company had been so used to me volunteering, that they were surprised that I actually wanted to play. I have to admit, I wasn't even sure I wanted to play!

I was worried I would look like a fraud, and that others would ask me golf related questions that I didn't know the answer to. So, I chose my team wisely. I chose ladies that were about as inexperienced as I was, and most importantly, each had a fantastic sense of humor. The night before the event, I received a call from one of the gals who worried that her chosen attire wouldn't suffice. For the most part, golf courses require a collared shirt to play. I encouraged her to wear any shirt that was comfortable with a collar. And you know what — she looked fabulous the next day. The four of us had lots of laughs and a wonderful time.

What I realized was that playing was a heck of a lot more fun and engaging for me than manning our company's table (or not even participating at all). It got me thinking about taking advantage of other opportunities that I had been putting off simply because I was afraid that I did not know enough to start.

*You've Got What It Takes*

Just like my daughter ordering and paying for something for the first time, or me putting together a team of non-golfers, you too have what it takes to play like the guys. The hardest part about getting started, is saying "yes."

All of us have talents that can be shaped and refocused in different ways. My educational and professional background is in marketing and public relations. The career path that I have achieved has led me into a variety of different jobs in various industries. All my positions had an underlying theme, which helped me accomplish an upward route to my career. Each new position I sought offered me challenges that I had not faced before. By relying on my core abilities, I was able to conquer new tasks and responsibilities with enthusiasm instead of fear.

What keeps you from saying "yes?" Is it fear of failure, other time commitments, or lack of interest? Try journaling your answer to the question:

"I want to _____, but I am unable to because of _____."

I want to:

_____

_____

_____

_____

_____

_____

_____

These three components play into each other quite often and ramp up our negative response ratio rather quickly. If you are not interested in something, then you definitely won't give it a try. I hear the excuse from people all the time that they just do not have enough time, when their real answer is, they are not interested. The same answer plays when fear is involved. How many of us do not think we can do something because it would be too much of a sacrifice to get there?

Whether golf is your thing or not, I hope that this book leads you to get out of your comfort zone, find the time, and jump into something new.

A friend of mine was asked to coffee by a woman who wanted to gain her business. Upon meeting at the coffee shop, the woman host paid for their drinks and asked to have them "to go." My friend was confused, and asked "I thought we were having a meeting here over coffee?" The other gal answered, "well, we are going to have coffee, but I thought it would be more fun to have coffee while getting a pedicure." These two ladies were able to have a good business conversation, over coffee, while engaging in an enjoyable activity together — and it only took one hour!

If you are truly not a golfer, don't worry about it. There are many other ways to enjoy work/life integration, and I encourage you to seek them out.

*You don't have to be great to get started, but you do need to start to be great.*

**CHAPTER 3**

# *Finding the (Cart) Path*

*"If all this talk of hobbies is making you think of the one sport through which deals are made, you are correct: You need to learn how to play golf. You don't have to be good, but you have to be competent enough to be invited for quality bonding time."* —Julie Steinberg (WSJ)

THERE IS SOMETHING about driving a golf cart that brings out the kid in you. It is a small, zippy vehicle, no doors with the capacity to drive on the grass. Who wouldn't want to have a little fun?

Golf courses install miles and miles of asphalt and concrete to guide us through the course. These darling sidewalks roll through the beautiful landscapes and take you to your ball's destination. Occasionally, the course design leaves you with a bit of confusion as to which way to turn.

I have taken wrong turns many times and have ended up everywhere but at the next tee box.

What if there wasn't a path? No signs, no indication of the start or the end. What would you do? Would you keep playing?

"Isn't it fun to go out on the course and lie in the sun?"
Bob Hope

Upon entering my freshman year of college, I had a plan. I was a young, determined, independent woman who was entering into a new life phase. I had enrolled in classes that would steer me towards my intended major of Pre-Med. I was living by myself (with a roommate) for the first time. I was single, so no boyfriend back at home could talk me into deviating from my plan. I was a strong student academically, and the classes I chose seemed more exciting than intimidating.

Then came organic chemistry. For the first time in my life, I failed a class. Failed with a big fat F. I felt as if I had left the cart path and broken the cart. My organized plan was smashed to pieces, and it was a jolt to my system. Sure, I could have retaken the class, but my heart just was not in it. I had encountered something that I had no passion for and could not force my brain into conquering it. It was time for a new path.

When you have a plan in place, and it appears in every way that it is a solid plan, how do you react when that plan falls apart?

_____

_____

_____

_____

_____

_____

_____

Like learning to play golf, I went looking for what felt right. I searched for a major that brought out something in me that I enjoyed doing but challenged me. I thought back to high school and considered what activities I enjoyed the most. I played sports, played a couple of musical instruments, but it was my experience on the Debate Team that pushed me outside of my comfort zone.

Being on the Debate Team created an adrenaline rush for me. When I was in that space, I experienced the most exhilarating feeling in the world. Rock musicians get it, as do professional athletes. They crave that experience again and again; and for some, it becomes the stimulant of their creativity and success. Public speaking was that stimulation for me. The nervous energy that I felt when getting up to speak in front of a crowd was quickly transformed into a state of power. I felt alive in a way that I had only experienced when participating in a sporting event. Public speaking and debate provided me with the drive to further my education.

I admire individuals who have found their passion. When they share it with you, their eyes light up. They appear at ease and know when and how to act. I've always wondered if somewhere along the way, someone gave them the magic tools they needed to succeed. I've even asked people what their biggest influence was, and for the most part, it turns out to be a bunch of little things. What sticks out as a common theme amongst all of them is they took advantage of opportunities right in front of them. Those opportunities didn't look like opportunities at first, and some of them were borderline opportunities at best. Much of creating your life's passions are the result of trying out something new, meeting new people, and putting yourself out there to give it a whirl.

Have you experienced seeing someone in the right role at the right time? A number of years ago, I had just joined a local business networking group. I joined because it seemed like the right thing to do to further my outreach and networking. The luncheon and casual meeting conversations I had with other business contacts were good, but what opened my eyes was the person who was leading the group. Each year, this organization appointed a volunteer business representative to chair the networking committee. It was a significant commitment, with facilitating a monthly luncheon, and smaller public presentations throughout the month.

As I became more acquainted with this group, I began to take more notice of the woman who was the chair that year. What stood out for me wasn't the fact that she was a good and confident public speaker, but it was how she eloquently responded to a negative occurrence. Just hours before a scheduled luncheon, some downsizing occurred within the business organization. The individuals who were laid off were very respected and liked in our community. Needless to say, the business community was infuriated. They were threatening to cancel their memberships and were out for blood.

Then, something miraculous happened. This woman (the chair) stepped up in front of everyone and shared what we needed to hear. She brought the room back together and bonded us as a stronghold to move forward in a positive way. I was in awe. That took guts, quick thinking, and a more than genuine positive attitude to walk into the fire and come out as everyone's hero.

That experience caused a shift in me to seek out opportunities that were challenging. I know that this woman chair grew immensely that day. I have had the pleasure to become her friend and see her conquer even more challenges. She is someone who I now consider a mentor and has provided me with a valued perspective on when to jump and when to wait.

Women have the ability to see distance. They can visualize and plan in great detail the outcomes they desire. So, what is holding us up from getting the results we want? We second guess whether we are on the right path. Too often, I see women talking themselves out of a positive action. I see the excitement of a new idea building, and their eyes light up. As they continue on and encounter obstacles, many times the fire in them starts to go out. The excuses bubble up, and they find ways not to go for it. I hear things like "I didn't have enough time" or "I need to do ___ first," and on and on. If you really want to do something, you will find the time, and you will figure it out. The cruel reality is that no one is going to do it for you. There will be many people there to help you on the way, but when it gets right down to it, the work is yours and yours alone.

What can you start doing right now as a baby step to your goals? I want you to think microscopic. Is it putting a list together? Is it researching what is available in your field or area? Is it having a conversation with someone?

_____

_____

_____

_____

_____

_____

_____

*Where Are the Signs?*

Many of us get lost along the way to finding our path. Sometimes, I wish my life path was illuminated for me like the flag on the green at the end of each hole. That way, I could size it up along the way. The sand traps would be easily identified, and the water hazards avoided. The greens would be immaculately manicured to the point that even the slightest rise or fall to the landscape provides me with the information one needs to shoot straight. As I get ready to drop the ball in the hole, I would have my trusted caddy with me to give some final words of wisdom.

Here is my golf and life reality. I study the layout of the course, put together a plan of action, and watch it all fall to pieces when I slice the ball on the first swing. What should I do? What would you do?

Look back at those baby steps you just wrote down. What is the next step for you?

_____

_____

_____

_____

_____

When failure is upon you, you have several choices. The easy way out: quit, pack up your clubs, and go home. You will avoid potentially embarrassing yourself over and over again. You will remain fresh and sweat free, and you won't have to get out of your comfort zone. Doesn't this sound exciting?

Write about a time you quit something in your life and how it made you feel?

_____

_____

_____

_____

_____

_____

_____

Option two: have a do-over (or a mulligan in the golf world). Preparation is valuable. You did your homework. You practiced beforehand. You identified your obstacles and made a plan of action about how to overcome them. Even the most prepared, most studied individuals slice the ball every once in a while. A few small tweaks to your beginning may be all it takes to get off on the right foot. Take a deep breath, focus, and relax. Hit it again.

Write down a time you did a do-over.

_____

_____

_____

*Finding the (Cart) Path*

_____
_____
_____
_____
_____

Option three: go after it. Being a golfer who slices the ball more than not, I have had my fair share of this experience. An experienced golfer will be upset when they slice the ball, especially when they know exactly what caused them to slice. Try to look for the positives in your shortfalls. If you sliced the ball, consider the distance that your ball traveled and how much closer you may be to the green. This most likely will cause you to readjust your game plan for that hole, but you may come out ahead in the long run.

Write down a time when you went after it.

_____
_____
_____
_____
_____

# GOLFING IN HEELS

I don't have the type of voice that carries very far. If I am trying to get the attention of an audience without a microphone, I cross my fingers and shout as loud as I can. I have tried to perfect a loud whistling sound for this purpose, but my mouth does not want to cooperate. Even if I have the undivided attention of a crowd, without assistance, it is difficult to hear my voice from the back of the room.

I was preparing to make a presentation to a large group a number of years ago at an event held in a restaurant. Needless to say, the acoustics in the restaurant were not favorable. It was loud in there and was even difficult to hear the person sitting next to you. When it was my turn to talk, I looked for the microphone I had been promised and was told that it had been forgotten. Not a good situation for the soft talker. I had to think fast and still create the same outcome I had planned for — which was to garner the groups' attention and effectively communicate the objectives of the organization I was representing in a clear and concise manner.

I quickly looked around my surroundings and found a solid chair to stand on. I am also vertically challenged, and the chair put me up about 2 feet higher than everyone else in the room. This allowed my voice to carry better, and the rough acoustics of the room worked for me from this height. I still had to raise my voice a bit and try not to let its pitch get too high, but I got their attention. As I called the group to order, their heads swung around and up to look at me.

What I was lacking in the volume of my voice, I gained in the physical presence of my body. At a higher level, the participants were able to see my face, even from the back of the room. I was able to make eye contact with everyone and gained their attention immediately and held it throughout my presentation. I went after it, and my unexpected "slice" turned into a "hole in one."

*Getting Back on Track*

Being off course feels pretty crummy. Your energy is low, your outlook bleak, and it is difficult to summon up the energy to dig in and get going. Getting out of a slump like this can take some time. You can practice and try and try again, with patience not always on your side.

When I'm in this position, I revert to something that I know I can do well. It's a simple thing I do, and although it could be considered a somewhat mundane activity, it instantly lifts my spirits and provides me with the gratification I am craving.

What is this activity, you ask? I clean and organize. Nothing lifts my spirits better than going through my entire wardrobe, basement, and kitchen cabinets to thin out and spruce up. It is not the activity itself that is therapeutic but the end result. When I am finished organizing, scrubbing, and polishing to a shine those areas of my house that need some TLC, I feel like I am floating on air. I have even been known to walk wistfully around my house and gaze at those spic and span areas and smile to myself for a job well done.

If you think for a minute that I am going to come over to your house and clean it for you so you can experience this sense of gratification — think again. I cannot give you this feeling. It is something you only achieve on your own. If cleaning isn't your "thing," than find some other activity. Maybe it's art, gardening, or spending time with a loved one. Make it something that grounds you and satisfies your soul. When you find your center, you will be able to get back on the path. Fine tune the skills that lift your spirit to their maximum potential.

What activities light you up inside?

_____

_____

_____

_____

_____

_____

_____

Take it a step further. What activities you listed above can be done anywhere at any time?

_____

_____

_____

_____

_____

_____

_____

These are the skills to keep in your back pocket for those times when you need to get back on the (cart) path.

**CHAPTER 4**

# *Gimme Gimme*

*"Golf is played by twenty million mature American men whose wives think they are out having fun." —Jim Bishop*

**WHEN YOUR WORLD** is synchronized, everything seems to go your way. Hitting every green light while driving down a street or discovering a windfall of extra cash in your checking account because you qualified for a discount makes everyone's day brighter. Life can be easier for you if you take it all in stride.

A *gimme* in golf is one of these added bonuses. You are so close to the hole that there is no possible way you can miss, so you just pick up your ball and be done with it. In this instance, there is no reason to putt again. Save your energy for the next hole.

For years, I have challenged myself on how to determine when to continue and when to quit. Being a perfectionist, I want to make sure any task I engage in is done not only right, but done to my high expectations. In doing projects in this manner, I have been disappointed that others do not notice my extraordinary work more often. I know they appreciate the fine-tuned, organized, and articulate presentations and projects I put together, but they don't always give me the recognition that I crave for putting in the extra effort.

So, why do I continue to do this? Will the extra push payoff in the end?

When my oldest child turned one, I threw a large family birthday party. The invitations were handmade, as were the cake and decorations. I was up until the wee hours of the night before prepping the house for the special day. I even remixed the icing for the cake three times to get the perfect shade of purple.

Then the big day was here. My thirty plus family members arrived with hugs, kisses, and an overload of presents for my little one. They were all excited to be a part of her first birthday, as was my daughter. As we blew out her candle, trashed the living room with wrapping paper, and snapped hundreds of pictures, not one comment was made about the purple frosted cake I had made. I realized at that moment, that the grayish purple icing that I had created during the first try would have sufficed and saved me hours of sleep.

At the end of the day, I was exhausted. I mean bone-tired exhausted, run-over-by-a-truck exhausted. The day was a complete success, but my daughter, and all of our loving family would have been just as happy with a thrown together party. They just wanted to be together and didn't care about the details.

*"Don't let the perfect be the enemy of the good."* —Voltaire

I hear excuses come out of women's mouths on an almost daily basis. They give excuses for being late, for not having a good hair day, and for why they can't do things that are not on their list of "I can do this task in my sleep" approved items. I sometimes wonder why they make it so hard, so hard to say "no" and even harder to say "yes."

The one lesson I have learned from golf is that you cannot try too hard. Being a female, I do not carry the same muscle mass as a male, and thus do not have the capacity to drive the ball as far as the guys. I used to think if I gave it everything I had and summoned the most power I could before making contact with the ball, than the distance I desired would be achieved. I could work on the aim later. Turns out, this way of thinking works only a small percentage of the time. The rest of the time, the ball goes 1) nowhere or 2) way far away into the great unknown never to be seen again. If I had to choose which method to use, I would go with a slow and even swing.

How do you achieve the easy strokes? Practice for one, and mental preparation for the rest.

As a young adult getting started in my career, I was anxious to move ahead quickly. I wanted my peers and superiors to value my opinion and take what little experience I had as a positive component of what I could bring to an employer. This is a tough dynamic to master when you are also in the learning phase.

For the past several years, I have had the tables turned on me. Instead of being the one to go after the business, I have been the prospective client for a number of salespeople. Most of these salespeople are young and inexperienced, as I once was. Needless to say, I enjoy meeting with them and try to fight back a cringe or two when their over-anxious presentations get to be too much.

One particular young lady made an impression on me. This gal was a college junior working as part of a marketing sales force during her summer break. She first visited my office to inquire about the decision maker she wished to meet with. After being given my business card by a fellow associate, she called me up and asked very nicely for a time to meet with her at my office. I accepted, and she arrived five minutes early for the set appointment. When I went out to the lobby to meet her, I was a bit shocked. This friendly, polite, professional young woman was not what I expected at all.

Her long locks were bleached too blonde, with some not so subtle red highlights. Her make-up would do well in a club, and her outfit would be sure to get at least ten dates upon her exit from my office. I did compliment her on her shoes, as I had a similar pair.

She sat herself down across from my desk and proceeded to present me with a very thorough sales pitch for the marketing package she was selling. We ended up chatting for a short while about her major, her career aspirations, and her background. We found we had a lot in common. I really liked this girl, but didn't have the heart to tell her (and possibly offend her) that her outside appearance did not measure up to her inward professionalism.

Here is where she knocked my socks off. A few days later, she followed up with me (as she said she would). After we handled the business transaction details of her sale, she asked me if she could ask me a question. "Shoot," I said. She asked me how I got the position I currently had because I made an impression on her and she wanted to garner any advice I had to give.

I rattled off my career history, including a college internship that helped to land me my first job out of school. I shared with her the need for networking and getting involved in the community. She then very candidly asked me "what do you think of my outfit?" I was secretly hoping we would be able to discuss that, and I was impressed she asked. The conversation we had that day was a positive one. I could tell that when she left my office, she had a determined outlook that I hope allowed her to shine inside and out.

This young woman was brave enough to ask me questions even though she had no idea if she would receive constructive criticism or just plain criticism. I was proud of her for putting herself out there to ask for feedback.

So many times, we have no idea if we are doing it the right way, but we are afraid to ask. I do not think I have ever played on a golf course that had rules posted for all to see and read. There is usually a sign with the number of the hole and the distance to the pin, but never in my experience a step by step guide on how to play. Needless to say, I have been afraid to ask for fear of sounding inexperienced.

The goal here is to make it easy: make it easy to ask for help, make it easy to be inquisitive, and make it easy to enjoy yourself and your surroundings —especially on the golf course.

> *"To play well you must feel tranquil and at peace. I have never been troubled by nerves in golf because I felt I had nothing to lose and everything to gain."* —Harry Vardon

*Create Your Own Fan Club*

Social media has allowed us to become fans of anyone or anything public or private. With the click of the mouse, we have signed up, joined the group, and reposted messages of those we admire over and over again. We look forward to the next thing that is shared and support it fervently with smiley faces and "likes."

What have people said about you lately? Would you be able to receive a favorable recommendation that was unsolicited just for being you?

Take a minute to jot down what a recommendation for you would say.

_____

_____

_____

_____

*Gimme Gimme*

People love to be liked. It not only makes them feel good, but it brings positive interactions and opportunities their way. My first experience with a true fan club was in the mid-1980's. My good friend was the youngest of five siblings and was exposed to a unique variety of music thanks to her older brothers and sisters. One group in particular, INXS, (and especially lead singer Michael Hutchence) was her favorite. She wrote to the INXS Fan Club and thanked them for producing great music. She even supplied a return envelope and asked for Michael's autograph. To her surprise, she received the singer's signature, and it was one of her most treasured possessions. She continued to write to their Fan Club regularly and used her special stationary to show her love and support for the positive impact that they had on her young life.

With her expression of dedication to this music group, and with their response to validate her support, INXS had a fan for life. She would tell anyone who would listen about their great music and encourage others to buy a tape (precursor to the Compact Disc and iTunes). What a better way to generate record sales than through loyal fans.

Even though I'm not the talented musician that I dream I would be (ok, I don't actually dream about this since I can't sing very well, but you get the point), I see the value in generating a fan base. Fans can be your family, friends, colleagues, or people you have done business with. They are the ones who would show up to support you if asked and make great references. So, how do you encourage their positive referrals when no activity is there to push them into action?

My first call to action:<br>
Promote others

A few years ago, I was volunteering with a charitable organization and was assisting with their annual fundraising activities in my area. Most fundraisers I have attended over the years involve either a meal, auction, or sporting event. This charity was geared towards women, so the main fundraising event was a luncheon. The funds raised each year had remained the same, and the committee was looking for creative ways to enhance the donations.

I thought about it, considered many of the other fundraising events that I had attended, and realized that we ladies were missing the boat on one event in particular, golf. In my experience, charity golf tournaments raise a bunch of money, but are played by mostly men. I knew there had to be a way to encourage all of these women philanthropists to get more involved with golf to enhance an already successful initiative.

I launched the first women-only golf fundraiser in my area. Knowing that many women weren't golfers (or had even been on a golf course let alone picked up a golf club), I created a golf clinic instead of a tournament.

The name of the game for this event was to raise money, so I had the challenge of trying to figure out how to give a professional lesson to many women non-golfers, and ask them to donate to a charity to have the experience. I called first upon a friend of mine who owned a golf shop in town. He was interested in getting in front of women because they are the ones who make most of the buying decisions in his store. To sweeten the deal, I asked him if he would be willing to be a guest golf pro and teach at the putting green. He agreed and used this event as an opportunity to not only showcase his golf store, but to also highlight his new putter line TallFace Putters™.

I needed a way to generate interest in women who might participate in this event, and I first needed some solid names to back me up. By starting with the obvious (a golf store) and using the commitment I had from them to generate others, I gained the momentum I needed to make this event work. I leveraged the in-kind donations that the guest golf pros gave me with lots of free publicity and connectivity to their prospective target market.

As a result, we not only successfully introduced many women to the game of golf, but we also increased the donations and support for the charity fundraiser. Through this charity golf event, I made some new friends and contacts and learned many new skills. It was definitely an eye-opening experience and started me thinking about writing this book.

My second call to action:
Share honest and genuine feedback

One of the easiest ways to put a smile on someone's face is to give them a compliment. The trick is that the compliment must be completely genuine. You couldn't compliment someone on her outfit if it looked like she scraped it off the floor that morning and didn't bother to wash or press it. Likewise, a compliment on something they obviously had nothing to do with (like giving someone a "way to go" for a project that they didn't work on) is stretching too far and comes across as lame.

If you want to become someone's fan, and in turn create a fan for yourself, you need to find some common ground. Paying special attention to their interests and goals gives you an edge in finding some ways to move forward together. I guarantee that every single person you meet has at least one thing in common with you. It may not be obvious at first or second glance, but if you dig a little deeper, the connection will surface.

I received some remarkable feedback from an acquaintance years ago that hit home with me. I had called this person to get their take on a volunteer opportunity in which they had been involved with in the past. I genuinely complimented their hard work with the initiative, as others had raved about the leadership and guidance this person illustrated. The reason for my call was to see if they thought I would be a good fit for the same opportunity. What was the feedback? I was advised that I would do a great job in that role, but my time would be better spent engaging in other activities where I could be seen in a more productive light. Prior to my conversation with this person, I hadn't even considered this angle. I initially had reached out to find out if I was capable of taking on this new responsibility and ended up with a fan who encouraged my movement in a better direction.

My third call to action:<br>
Be their biggest fan

Choosing how to spend your time takes a delicate hand. As women, we tend to say "yes" to more things than we can handle. One result of our over commitment is that it can appear to others like we are not putting forth a full effort, and no one wants to appear as if they are slacking off. Committing to something that seems like a favor to a friend when you know full well that you won't be able to provide the time, service, or skill that they are requesting sets them and you up for failure.

To be a true fan, only commit to requests that you can support 100%, or communicate what level you can participate at from the get-go. Much respect is given to those who respectfully decline invitations, versus those who accept but do not follow through. Be your best self with others' endeavors, and they will be their best for you.

In addition to not being a golfer, I am also not a cook. Oh sure, I can whip up a boxed mix of brownies any day to cure a chocolate fix. However, if you ask me to make a homemade anything for an event, then I will either offer to do something else to help or call the nearest caterer.

When my oldest child entered preschool, I was excited for her to meet new friends. I was also excited to meet the other parents and hopefully forge some new friendships. During my daughter's first year of preschool, she was invited to many birthday parties for her classmates. I hadn't even considered throwing a classmate party for my then three-year-old, but we accepted the invitations anyway. Walking in the door to the first of these parties, I was astounded at the level of celebration that these parents had put together for their little tot. There were rented bounce houses, decorations all over the house, and cupcakes that could have graced the cover of a magazine. I asked the hostess where she purchased the cupcakes. When she said "oh these? I just made them last night," I thought, What?!?!? You mean to tell me that this busy working mother just whipped up these little treats all by herself and didn't even look the least bit frazzled when some of my fellow party guests were smearing the frosting all over her carpet!

She sure made a fan of me that day. The party was an absolute delight, but I felt a big lump of fear rise in me as the day went on. How in the world was I supposed to live up to this kind of party? Do three-year- old children expect this level of detail? Do their parents?

My husband and I made a decision that day to not hold a friend or classmate birthday party until our children reached their fifth birthday. That decision did take a weight off my shoulders, at least for a couple more years. But what was I to do when the fifth birthday was upon us?

*If you're going to sweat the small stuff, come prepared.*
    The way we react to negative situations is different for each and every one of us. Some of you non-golfers out there will just decline an invitation to participate in a golf event, instead of potentially making an embarrassment out of yourself. But there are those times when you are forced to participate — even though you'd rather run the other direction.
    I live in Kansas, and we typically have triple-digit summertime temperatures. With it being the Midwest, we also typically have below-freezing winters, which make for a lovely showing of the seasons, and only a few months to squeeze in a lot of outdoor events. Several summers ago, I was participating in a golf event that my company was sponsoring. I had what I thought were the essentials: golf clubs, comfy shoes, golf balls, tees, etc. What I completely didn't think about was how my body would feel after five hours in the blistering sun. I did not bring any sunscreen or a water bottle. The beverage cart offered some refreshment, but the day became a brutal test of my mental and physical capabilities.
    Then something marvelous happened. One of the ladies I was golfing with opened up her golf bag and took out ice cold washcloths. She brought enough for our entire foursome, and it was the best relief from a hot and exhausting day I

had ever experienced. Her little bit of preparation allowed us to get through the day.

When you are faced with new situations, preparing effectively can be difficult. Should you bring snacks, drinks, and a change of clothes for every member of your family? Do you have room for all those extras? Do you really need them?

I am a fan of multi-tasking objects. Both of my children are out of diapers, but I will probably always carry around a pack of baby wipes in my car. They are perfect for spills, sticky fingers, and all-around car cleanliness. A friend of mine carries a couple of bath towels in her trunk. She swears by them to use as makeshift blankets, muddy shoe pads, and to get that spot free shine after a car wash. Neither of these items take up a lot of room nor are they expensive.

The lesson of this chapter is to make things easier. We may not always know the easiest route to take at first, but there are signs all around us about what to do. Take heed from others who have gone before you and choose the path that works for you. No one has the best answer for everything. Only you can decide what is most important, and what can truly be a gimme — even off the golf course.

**CHAPTER 5**

# Who's Your Caddy?

*"Men of a certain caliber have bespoke suits. Women tend not to be as conscious that dress is part of their professional brand," —Rand Kaspi of LawScope Coaching.*

SOME OF THE best teachers I have had were the ones who made learning not only fun, but made it look and feel easy. These teachers made me want to try a little harder and never made me feel bad when I failed. In the sixth grade, I had the opportunity to experience a teacher who made a remarkable impact on me. She absolutely amazed me. It was not what she taught (and in fact, I don't remember what subject she actually taught), but the method in which she created a learning environment. She was truly engaged with me and all her other students. The following school year, Ms. M and her family moved away, and she and I remained pen pals for years. For a sixth grader who only had Ms. M for one class, I was enamored of her efforts to connect with her students and hope that she knew what a positive impact that had on me.

In the game of golf, caddies are like your favorite teacher. They point you in the right direction but do not give you all the answers. They respond to your need for guidance by giving you that extra push before letting go — realizing that in the end it is all up to you.

Professionally, I have had the good fortune to work with some pretty amazing people, who in turn, came to be mentors. As a young adult, finishing my degree and starting my career, I found my first mentor. My first "big girl" job was as a sales executive. However much my college degree prepared me for this position academically, I was not quite prepared for the most important aspect of the job, dealing with and recruiting clients.

Women are dealt a mixed hand when it comes to business. We are expected to be attentive, but not overbearing; courteous, but not a push over; and aggressive without being a bitch. Then there is the art of making the sale, and what an art it is! My mentor expertly guided me through this minefield as I learned how to handle myself professionally.

One of the top attributes to consider is your appearance. I am not talking about how attractive you are, but how you present yourself. The saying "dress for success" is not to be taken lightly. For a woman to be taken seriously, she must have the physical presence to back it up. My mentor walked me through clothing choices and showed me how a well-tailored outfit can maintain your femininity, but also increase your respect level. A look with a bit of an edge can also be an asset. Throwing on a splash of color with something like a pair of red shoes with a classic black pencil skirt and a crisp white shirt sets up an aura of confidence.

You can walk down any street in any part of the world and instantly identify someone who is confident. They are holding their head up, their eyes are alert, shoulders back, and their walk is determined. Poise is something that can be learned. Even someone wearing sweatpants and an old t-shirt can have poise, but the combination of the dress and poise makes an invigorating result.

*The Shoes Make the Woman*

I am not a tall person. Standing only 5 ft. 4 inches, my dream is to be taller. To compensate, I wear heels almost everywhere I go. To me, height has its advantages. Despite this, several of my mentors have been women who were, ironically enough, shorter than I. They mastered the art of creating a commanding presence from their petite statures.

How do they do it? They pay special attention to the other aspects of their presence. In addition to wearing clothes that fit them well (and this does not mean you have to spend a fortune on your wardrobe — you just need to discover, or have someone help you discover, what works for you), they carry themselves with distinction.

My earliest mentor gave me a good piece of advice: Always make sure your shoes look new. You can be wearing a freshly pressed, well fitted business suit that you got for a steal on sale, one that makes you look and feel like a million bucks, but if your shoes are worn out and scuffed, you might as well put on sweatpants.

*Sphere of Influence*

A caddy connects your weaknesses to others' strengths. On the golf course, caddies exploit your strengths to move you ahead faster, while downplaying your weaknesses.

Do you know what you do well? I'm not asking about what you like to do, although they might be one and the same. I know that for myself, if I can relax and make good contact with the ball, then my drive is the strongest part of my game. I would have to say that my short game is my weakness. Knowing this about myself helps me look to others who can balance my game and teach me something new.

> *Many women make the mistake of seeking sponsorship from only the people above them. Some of the people you work with are going to be in charge and could help you rise in the ranks. —Julie Steinberg*

Personal growth can happen on a variety of levels. You may set out on a specific course, complete with action plans and goals, to gain a particular skill. You may fail miserably and discover something profound about your methods. You may encounter a challenge from a superior, adversary, or best friend that causes you to step out on a limb and go for it. All of these are learning processes that cause you to bend, shape, and mold yourself into something better.

Moving into my next job, I encountered an even different mentorship opportunity. This one was completely unexpected, and although not my strongest mentoring relationship, it provided me with much needed people skills. While still maintaining a sales position, my role was more that of a counselor than of a marketing advisor. I had to figure out how to bring forward and connect the industry that I represented with the rest of the community in a way that was proactive.

Here is where I discovered the power of my peers. To get a leg up, I needed to be engaged with others outside of my specialty. I needed to find out what made others tick before I could share with them the benefit of working with me. Networking became for me, and still is, a powerful strategy for information sharing, relationship building, and increasing overall business aptitude. I have found some of my best ideas are from unexpected meetings and conversations that happened just because I showed up to an event.

When you are faced with an unknown, how do you go about sharing it with others? Do you rattle off the facts you know? Do you point them to a website? Do you try to assimilate your task with something more familiar? Record your response below.

_____

_____

_____

_____

Identifying a need (yours or someone else's) can be a challenge. A good golf caddy will just sit back and watch you in motion for a while. They will see how you take your drives, line up your shorter shots, and respond to a difficult putt. Utilizing their observations and their recommendations on a club, angle, or hand position on the club can mean all the difference in how you perform.

When you are trying to get the attention of someone (a client, your child, or a perfect stranger) what technique works best?

Now, different circumstances, and audiences warrant different techniques. For example, if you see someone stepping out into a busy street where a car may hit them, you may shout, "Watch Out!" If you want a prospective client to meet with you for a potential business transaction, the shouting approach may not work to your advantage.

*Use Your Best Approach*

Think about the activities that you like to do best that get the biggest impact. Are you someone who enjoys small intimate gatherings, one-on-one meetings, or large group presentations? All three settings are great for meeting new people but each needs a different approach.

Your motivation and reason for the result can vary based on your audience. Just like in golf, you have a bag full of clubs that serve difference purposes.

Let's start with small intimate gatherings. Whether it be in your home, at a restaurant, or in your office's conference room, synergy amongst your guests is key. Taking the time to select your participants carefully for this setting will make your time together go much more smoothly. Consider the styles of the people in the room. Are some more apt to talk more freely? Are others quieter?

The purpose of your meeting will also dictate whom to include. If your goal is to gain support for a project, or to make a sale, having at least one person in the room who already supports your initiative is helpful. That person can be prepped beforehand and be called upon to be your advocate. Having allies in the room for a small gathering creates an extension of yourself that promotes a sense of belonging and acceptance and can go a long way to getting the others in the room to say "yes".

One-on-one meetings can take on a different strategy. This is where I like to make sure the meeting environment compliments the person. You do not want to take an introvert to a loud restaurant or a non-sports fan to a ball game. Doing some research on how they like to spend their time will go a long way in preparing for your meeting.

If your one-on-one meeting takes place at their office, find out who their colleagues are. Having common connections, or at least a name of reference, will put them (and you) much more at ease. One-on-one meetings can also be intimidating for you because you are the only one in the room and don't have others to help support your cause.

To start off your one-on-one meeting, keep in mind these helpful tips:

1. Maintain eye contact when you are talking, but most importantly, when they are talking. Eye contact shows acknowledgement and interest and creates an unspoken level playing field.
2. Keep your phone tucked away and silenced (or turned off). Your focus should be 100% on the person you are meeting with. Even having your phone on the desk or in your hand is a distraction. Be respectful of their time and communicate your total commitment to being there.
3. Allow the person you are meeting with to talk more than you. Ask open-ended questions that allow you to get to know them better and shows genuine interest in them, their company, and their goals.
4. Bring something to leave behind. If your meeting went well, and you want to continue the conversation and interaction at another time, provide them with something to remember you by. You can leave a supplement to your presentation with some

additional information, an invitation for a future meeting, or an invitation for a more social event.

And lastly, let us discuss large group presentations. I actually think that large groups are similar in nature to one-on-one meetings. Let me explain why. In large groups, you may think it is easy to not focus on one person, but in reality, you need to focus on one person at a time. The skill of maintaining eye contact with several different people as you give your presentation allows you to receive instant feedback. If the participants are willing to meet your eyes, then you can measure their level of interest in what you are saying by their facial expressions and body language. By looking at them, you are acknowledging their non-verbal feedback, and this can allow you to modify your presentation — especially if you are getting into the weeds with a lot of data.

Large group presentations also require you to talk more slowly. Large groups, with all eyes on you, can create anxiety and nervousness, which then may translate into an increased heart rate and a faster paced presentation. When I am in front of large groups, I tend to take several deep breaths right before I begin. This helps slow down my heart rate, and allows me to start off at a pace that is much more manageable.

Some additional tips for large group presentations include:
1. Leave room for air. You may think that taking a pause feels like an eternity. In reality, it is very natural.

Having some breaks in your speech or presentation allows for the audience to digest your words.
2. Smile, and use nonverbals to get buy in from your audience. In addition to eye contact, if you are presenting information to create support and even a sale, nodding your head and showing support yourself creates a mirror for your audience to follow.
3. Consider carefully your props. Props may be a podium, presentation materials, eyeglasses, or even your hands. What do you want your audience to focus on the most? What could be a distraction?

Similar to the approach shot in golf (where you are getting close to the hole), pulling out these helpful reminders for any size of setting can make it easier to get the win.

*Friendship versus friendliness*

Women are just so darn nice. They want to make you feel welcome, comfortable, and needed. They will cook for you, shop for you, and bend over backwards to show their appreciation. And I am talking about women in the workplace.

Women step up as the note takers, coffee fetchers, and organizers of the office party. They volunteer to decorate, delegate, and design the party invitations for events of all sizes.

What is their hope for all this hard work? That they will be seen as a hard worker, motivator, and most of all a good friend.

Have you ever been in that position? Have you raised your hand because your felt like it was up to you to take care of things?

_____

_____

_____

_____

_____

_____

Like a caddy on the golf course, women have a natural inclination to offer support for each other. In an article from *Science of People* by Vanessa Van Edwards, she shares how authors Barbara Annis and Richard Nesbitt examine gender differences in their book "Results at the Top: Using Gender Intelligence to Create Breakthrough Growth."

In regard to handling conflict, Annis and Nesbitt share that "Men tend to depersonalize and externalize issues or problems, giving them time to think through solutions, often in solitude. Women tend to personalize and are more inclined to talk through the issue to reach understanding."

Both genders have a valuable place in the workforce and can actually complement each other very well. Even if women are more emotional caretakers, we do not have to always step forward first to take on the friendship producing tasks.

Men, on the other hand, hold friendship to a different level. They do not immediately set out to recruit new friends. They sometimes sit back and let us ladies handle all the details, while they get to focus on the broader scope of what is to be accomplished. They provide a friendly environment in which to interact, and when asked, are happy to step up to any job.

What can we, as women, learn from this? Using your teammates or colleagues in a collaborative way can produce the results you desire. There are many ways to be impactful and create meaningful friendships without exhausting yourself. Letting others step up with ideas and then working within your own time frame and skill set to complement their efforts may create the best win-win for workplace success.

# CHAPTER 6

# *Drive*

*"What other people may find in poetry or art museums, I find in the flight of a good drive."* —Arnold Palmer

THE PREPARATION, THOUGHTS, and power that go into a good drive are intense. Annika Sorenstam (Retired LPGA golfer) decided a few years back that she wanted to play in a men's PGA event. She had the skill, (earning numerous titles herself and playing on the LPGA tour for years) but the question that fumbled around in her head was if she had the physical power to make her drives equal that of the men. To prepare herself, she spent months working with personal trainers and strength and conditioning coaches to build muscle mass. She needed the strength to drive the ball farther than she ever had before. Annika put herself through an amazing test of endurance (both physically and mentally) to even compete. In the end, she did not win the tournament, but she did prove — especially to herself — that she did have the drive.

I am always enamored by people who undertake great feats. They prepare, push, and stretch themselves into doing and being more than they currently are.

What is inside of them that makes them want to do these things? Write down some ideas below about great feats you have taken on.

_____

_____

_____

_____

_____

_____

_____

My friend, Holly Herman, became the CEO of a company at the young age of 32. How did she do this, you ask? She dug in, prepared herself, and seized an amazing opportunity that I think surprised even her. In learning about her story to the top, I realized that the major thing that stood between her and the rest of us is that she said "yes" even when she didn't feel 100% confident that she could do everything it would take to be a successful CEO.

*Drive*

She was, and is, confident in herself, and has the drive to jump and jump far.

Holly knew she had the skills, she knew that she could learn quickly, and most importantly, she knew that this new title of CEO would take her way outside of her comfort zone and catapult her into a new level of the business world. Being a female CEO, and being as young as she was, Holly had some definite challenges that she handled with finesse. The biggest challenge facing her was the company she was hired to run was failing.

> "Successful people have energy. They have found the key to increasing their energy levels and are able to sustain them even during difficult times. Have you ever met someone who is wonderfully successful and has low energy? Increasing your energy starts with eliminating those areas of your life that are energy drains." —Holly Herman

Her immediate challenge as a new CEO was to figure out a way to quickly turn around a failing organization. In Holly's case, her drive came from her ability to believe in several truths.
1. "You can make it up." There are not always a set of rules to follow, so create your own.
2. "It's ok to be scared."
   This is a common misconception that successful people thrive on. Fear and risk are part of life and businesses. No one knows all of the answers and

having a bit of the unknown present can create new opportunities that you need to explore.
3. "Follow your instincts."
There is something to be said about going with your gut. You can create spreadsheet upon spreadsheet of the black and white reasons why something will work. What you cannot always quantify is the impact those choices will have on a culture, overall strategy, or buy in. Your instincts will help take the data and guide you to what feels right.
4. "Surround yourself with incredible people."
Our ability to perform at a high level and achieve high goals with leaps and bounds are heightened by who is on our team. Utilizing others' strengths, for example, incorporating a phenomenal CFO that can organize your financials better than you ever could, will not only free you up to focus on other aspects of your organization's success but will move you forward faster.

Where does your drive come from? And how do you feel about risk?

_____

_____

_____

_____

To get started, you first must establish some momentum. Darren Hardy, author of *The Compound Effect*, places a lot of value on the power of creating momentum. Hardy uses the image of starting up a playground merry-go-round to illustrate his point. "The first step was always the hardest — getting it to move from a standstill. You had to push and pull, grimace and groan and throw your entire body weight into the effort." Through this example, Hardy explains how progress at first is slow, but once you decide to go for it and push yourself, maintaining momentum is much easier than starting.

Getting over the hump of inactivity can be exhausting. If where we wanted to go was as easy as pushing a merry-go-round, then we would all be ahead of the game. Sure, a few of us would not want to put forth the effort (and instead hop along for a ride), but a seemingly easy task like pushing a playground object around doesn't appear too daunting.

Think about what you fear the most and write it down below.

Public speaking tends to be at the top of most people's lists of what they fear most, as does flying, networking, and encountering snakes. Look back to see what you wrote down and think about what small tasks you can do to help you overcome your fear.

Mastering small tasks may be the key to your success, and the start to finding your drive.

I am a mother of two, and with two pregnancies comes unwanted post-baby fat. With both of my pregnancies, I had to work hard to get those last 10 pounds off. I was fortunate going into each pregnancy, as I had already established a healthy lifestyle. What I was unprepared for was the changes my body went through as a result of carrying a baby. When I went back to my normal routine of eating and exercising, it was not enough to get to where I wanted to be. I had some choices to make. I could either live with those extra 10 pounds or make some changes to get them off.

To get started, I went through my kitchen cupboards and refrigerator. I took a hard look at what I was eating. Anyone that knows me understands my sweet tooth addiction — especially when it comes to chocolate and frosting. Yum! I had to find a way to satisfy my daily sweet tooth cravings while lowering my calorie intake. I did a little research and found some lower calorie and healthier ways to work this into my diet. I then got rid of all the other junk that had worked its way into our home. No more full-fat ice cream, regular potato chips, or soda of any kind. I replaced these with non-fat frozen yogurt, baked chips, pretzels, whole grain crackers, and water, water and more water. Did some of these items taste different than their less-healthy alternatives? For a short while, but that's when my next motivator kicked in.

*The Power of Visualization*

After my first child was born, my husband and I booked a couples only trip to a tropical location. We booked the trip a good six months in advance, so I had plenty of time to get myself vacation ready. That promise of a kid-free vacation on a sunny beach was motivation for me to get back into shape. I had already started my fitness goals with some food choice changes, but I needed to add in an exercise component. I needed to move my body and needed to do it on a regular basis in ways that were different from my daily routine.

With baby in tow, I put my daughter in a stroller and took off on long walks. We both enjoyed the fresh air, and she got a new world to look at and explore while I got in some cardio. On bad weather days, I strapped her in a baby backpack carrier (or front carrier) and did work around the house. The extra weight from my baby gave my body that extra kick to burn and tone where I needed it most.

Starting with small efforts and doing them regularly, increased my success rate. If you think about your daily routine, what is one small thing you can change to improve yourself? Is it switching from soda to sparking water? Is it parking in the back of the lot when going to the grocery store to get in some extra walking?

Jot down those small things that you can start doing right now.

_____

_____

_____

_____

_____

How about taking an inventory of your closet? The power of visualization also applies to how you currently see yourself. Think about your favorite outfit. If it is your favorite, then I am going to assume that it makes you look fabulous, and you glow when you put it on. What if every piece of clothing you own made you feel as great as you do wearing your favorite outfit?

*Visualization exercise*

Complete these sentences:

I feel the most amazing when I

_____

_____

_____

_____

I love how I look when I

_____

_____

_____

    I am a clothes horse. I love to shop, and collect tops, skirts, dresses, pants, shoes, accessories — you name it. I love the changing of the seasons when a new line of fashions hits the stores. My biggest thrill is to find an amazing item on sale that really flatters my figure. The problem is, sometimes the thrill of the find masks the true appearance of an item on me. For example, I found a pair of designer jeans for $6 that I thought were gorgeous. I bought them and tried to find ways to wear them often. I hung onto these jeans for years.

When my husband said in a very sweet tone "honey, those pants really don't flatter your figure," at first I was taken back because I LOVED those jeans. They were designer. They were on sale. And, because of those two facts, my brain was mystified into thinking they must look good on my body.

My husband and I share a walk-in closet. It is a good size and plenty big enough to hold both of our wardrobes. My problem is that my side of the closet seems to grow at a much faster pace than his, and I am forced to either relocate or remove what doesn't fit. It is not an easy task for me to remove clothing items from my closet. I deliberate at length over what needs to go, and often times don't get rid of very much at all.

A friend of mine referred me to a wardrobe consultant to help with this quandary. At first, I was a little skeptical. What was this consultant like? Would she understand my tastes? Would she really know what looked good on me? Was she affordable? I am happy to report that she fulfilled all my needs and was very affordable.

I invited this consultant over during the holiday break a couple of years ago, and she and I spent two hours going through every piece of clothing I owned. Because I had never met her before, she was objective in her opinions and didn't take my personal attachment of items to heart. At the end of our time together, she had made a pile of approximately two-thirds of my wardrobe to get rid of. Some items had seen better days and were pilled, faded. or just worn out. Some items were the wrong fit for me — jackets that were too boxy, pants that were too fitted in the wrong places, and shirts that had an unflattering neckline for my body type.

She then gave me a list of suggested "do's" and "don'ts" for future shopping purchases. Her recommendation for structuring your wardrobe was this: If it does not absolutely flatter your figure and make you feel like a million bucks, then don't wear it. It's hard to come to these wardrobe decisions on your own, and I highly recommend either hiring a wardrobe consultant to help you, or enlist a trusted (and objective) friend whom you admire for their clothing choices.

Once you can visualize yourself on a daily basis looking and feeling great, you have just given your motivation a jump start.

*What's your 59?*

When Annika Sorenstam achieved 59, she used this record-breaking score to drive her success, including 72 LPGA tournament wins, 10 majors, and eight Player of the Year awards. She went on to establish the Annika Sorenstam Academy where this "question inspires attendees to share their life goals, which they can then pursue with the same degree of focus and determination that Sorenstam brought to the course on the day of her momentous accomplishment." – *Annika Sorenstam Academy*

Taking heed from Annika, what was the best success you ever had? Did you ace a test in school? Land the job of your dreams? Hit the winning run in a ball game? Think big!

## GOLFING IN HEELS

_____

_____

_____

_____

_____

_____

How did you feel when your "59" was accomplished? If I had to guess, I bet your answer will be something like: pure elation, ultimate clarity, and WAHOO!

Finding your drive, means connecting to the emotions and activities that bring forth your most positive outcome. Drawing from past successes helps us to set goals and move us forward to a big outcome.

**CHAPTER 7**

# *Conquering Fear*

*"I felt more equal on the golf course than in the workplace, they could see me as a 360-degree person."* —Pippa Woods

CLOSE YOUR EYES for a minute and picture a relaxing setting. I picture the beach, the sunny sky, the soft sand at my feet, and the sound of the rolling waves. I smell the salt from the ocean, the coconut oil from my sunscreen, and a sweet citrus fragrance from the icy drink I am sipping. The world could stand still for me at these moments, and I would be in heaven. When I visualize the beach, my imagination floods all my senses with comfort, warmth, and belonging.

A few weeks before traveling to my favorite tropical vacation spot, I stopped in at a local Mexican dive to pick up some take-out for dinner. When I opened the door, I was greeted with the warm smell of freshly made tortillas and the sweet smell of the margarita machine. I was instantly transported to my beloved beach and took a deep breath to engage my entire being in that experience. For that moment, I was transformed. My mind went instantly to the beach and brought up every sight, smell, taste, and sound that I encountered there. I felt immediately at ease. It could have been the fact that I was counting down the days until my vacation, but I was not expecting a quick stop at a restaurant to put those thoughts and feelings into my head.

When do you experience your favorite sensory setting? Can you close your eyes and put yourself there? Does a favorite song, smell, or food help?

_____

_____

_____

_____

_____

_____

Fear exists in all of us. Even the bravest, strongest people on earth experience fear. They may not show the telltale signs of this emotion, but it is there.

One of my favorite lessons on fear is from Eleanor Roosevelt. She asks us to

*"Do one thing each day that scares you."*

I found this quote a few years ago, and I read it every day. The "scary thing" that I do each day may not be comparable to climbing Mount Everest or jumping through a ring of fire, but nonetheless, it takes an extra bit of gumption for me to give it a whirl. The fear that I experience, however small, is real. It makes my heart beat a little faster, my palms sweat, and my mouth go dry.

*"Character cannot be developed in ease and quiet. Only through experience of trial and suffering can the soul be strengthened, ambition inspired, and success achieved."*
—Helen Keller

I asked my daughter on the way home from school one day if she did anything that day that scared her. She surprised me when she said, "I asked the new girl if she would like to sit next to me at lunch." I asked her why she did that, and her response was "Mom, she was looking around and no one was talking to her. I felt really bad for her." I prodded further and asked her why she spoke up. She said, "I didn't want to at first, but I thought how I would feel if no one talked to me on my first day at a new school." Needless to say, I was so proud of my daughter for conquering her fear.

She then turned the tables on me and asked me the same question of "what did I do today that scared me?" I had to think about that for a minute. As adults, we do so many of the "have to's" that we either brush the fear aside quickly or try to figure out a solution to our needs without ever having to embrace fear.

If talking to strangers is a fear for you, there are plenty of ways to avoid them all together. You could shop for everything (including your groceries) online and have them delivered to your house. You could always communicate via email or text message to avoid any interaction, or you could bring along a trusted friend or associate to be your "wing man" for those events you cannot possibly avoid.

Now I am going to turn the tables on you. What is one thing you did today that scared you?

_____

_____

_____

_____

_____

_____

I have heard from women hundreds of times in this past year who say that they cannot play golf. I hear plenty about how women do not play golf, but I hear more often the "can't" word. That makes me think that fear is definitely a factor.

When we see someone as an expert at something, we are either drawn to them, or pulled away. In the case of golf, I see more people intimidated by others who appear to be experts, but who are actually just people who have an understanding of the game and are out to have fun. Now, there are some who are out for the win, but for the most part, the element of fun overrides their skill.

I have always been a believer that knowledge is the key to developing yourself and your relationships. I have engaged in many situations where I did not know a thing about what was being discussed. What is the best way to learn about new things? Start asking questions. Everyone loves to talk about themselves, or about what they are knowledgeable and passionate about. By asking questions about the topic at hand, you are not only gathering information for yourself, but you are also pumping that person up by engaging them in what matters most to them.

Have you ever been in a room full of people, and noticed a few loners who either hug the wall, or don't leave their seat? This maybe you I am describing, so you get the idea. Pick those people to talk to first. They are ripe for the picking and are probably scared to death of approaching others. By introducing yourself and asking some simple "get to know you" questions, you just opened yourself up to conversations with all the people who are working the crowd better than you.

*Remember that the past does not equal the future*

If you have ever played golf and missed every swing, then your attitude towards the game is probably to never try it again. I played in a private golf tournament recently entertaining some clients. I played horribly. I whiffed several of my shots and only got the ball on the green a couple of times throughout the 18-hole course. How miserable! Luckily, one of the players I was with brought her "A" game and carried us through to make just over par.

I am not a strong player but tend to have some strong shots. I wrote this game off as just one of those bad days.

> *There is no such thing as a "run of bad luck." The reason people believe such nonsense is that the human brain creates patterns out of random events and remembers the events that fit the pattern. —Geoffrey James (INC.com)*

So, where does "bad luck" play into our fears? If we take heed of what Mr. James is saying, then we can blame our brain for the patterns created by our bad experiences. To retrain our brain takes practice and lots of positive experiences that create new patterns.

*What Scares You the Most*

My biggest fear is failure itself. I fear it so much, that many times I stay away from activities when I am not sure that I will do well. For example, I am not a great singer. I sang in the church choir growing up and sing to the radio in the car, but I don't think anyone would applaud my musical abilities if I had to go it alone.

At a company retreat a number of years ago, I was asked to take part in a creative presentation to highlight the successes for the past year. "Sure!" I said, honored to be included in the presentation. I soon discovered that the presentation would include singing and my fear level started to rise. To add fuel to the fire, the presentation was changed up the night before the deadline. In fact, I had about an hour to learn a song. Needless to say, I was not a happy camper. In that hour of prep time, the organizers wanted all of us to practice in front of each other. I politely declined and promised to make them proud.

Walking to the stage, I had never felt more nervous and sicker to my stomach. I told myself that it was only two minutes of my life, and I just needed to give it my all. So, I took a deep breath, and went for it.

When it was all over, I did get a few laughs, and even laughed at myself. That definitely was an experience that I would not want to repeat, but I made it through.

*We gain strength, and courage, and confidence by each experience in which we really stop to look fear in the face... we must do that which we think we cannot. —Eleanor Roosevelt*

When you stop to think of the things you most want to accomplish in life, do you stop because of fear? Your fear can manifest as not having enough information, not knowing how to start, or most commonly, fear of failure.

As you work your way through this book, I have asked you to write down many kinds of reflections relating to fear. I now want you to focus on the phrase:

What is stopping you?

_____

_____

I started to think about writing a book over ten years ago. My writing started first as journaling. Getting my thoughts down on paper and forming them into a cohesive story posed a challenge to me. I was not a strong English student in school and had to force myself to write numerous research papers that didn't yield high marks. My past writing experience told me that I was not a strong writer and prompted the question, why would I ever want to pursue writing a book?

When I turned 30, I composed some thoughts about my then milestone birthday. At first, I thought, who in the world would want to read something about my so-so existence? I decided to read my composition to the members of my Book Club. Here is what I wrote:

I used to think that being thirty was old. When you're 6 years old, and helping your Mom make a birthday cake for your Dad's 39th birthday, you think "Wow, he's almost 40!" Where does the time go?

Thirty. For some people, that is half of their life, for others, only a third. I hope mine is the latter. As I embark on the third decade of my life, I reflect on what I have accomplished thus far. I have gotten through school, completed college (in seven years instead of four), got married, bought two houses, traveled to Europe, and had a baby. If you look at it that way, I have sure done a lot. I've also changed jobs six times since college, racked up a lot of debt (and paid most of it off), learned to balance my career and family, and realized that it takes two people earning a decent salary to live comfortably today.

Thirty-year-olds tend to compare their accomplishments to others. Well, I'm sure people at any age compare themselves to others, but a thirty-year-old is stuck between the youth of their twenties and the maturity of being a real adult. When you tell people that you are in your twenties, it seems that you are always younger and less experienced than someone else. But thirty brings more sense of accomplishment, even if you do not have many accomplishments. When you tell people you are in your thirties, a sense of understanding and admiration blooms inside you and inside them.

What are all the other thirty-year-olds doing with their lives? I am sure not all of them have found the answers they have been looking for in life. I don't think there is a magical age when all of life's conquests have been fulfilled, but I do believe that understanding of such things comes with time.

As I approach my thirtieth birthday, I am not sad to be leaving my twenties behind. At the gym today, I noticed some college girls on the Stairmaster. What I would not give for the legs and behind of a twenty-year-old! Their skin is so smooth, their energy is limitless, and they can eat whatever they want and still look like Barbie dolls. Although I am a mere ten years older than these girls, there is a difference in our appearance. I am fortunate to have a healthy figure, but that figure has changed somewhat over the years. I am not the muscular and cellulite-free girl I once was and now lovingly carry around that little pouch of flabby stomach skin that was created by the birth of my wonderful daughter. So, I try to accentuate those attributes that can look like a twenty-year-old. I have great hair and full lips. I can use concealer and moisturizer to hide the fine lines that have been creeping up around my eyes. I buy tailored clothes that compliment my figure; and best of all, I use my knowledge and maturity to be a fun and witty person.

A friend once told me, "your twenties are spent trying to figure out what you want to do, your thirties are spent getting there, and your forties are spent enjoying your success." She is 42. If our thirties are to be spent getting to the place we have recently discovered, how will we know when we have reached that place? Will financial success by that mark? Will it be a certain level of job status? Can we enjoy our success before 40?

When I look at friends of mine who are in their thirties, I see some differences in the way they view success. I only have a few friends that are married, and most of the ones that are do not have any children. They are mostly career-focused people with aspirations to achieve the status of parenthood sometime later. "I'll have a child someday," they tell me.

There have been countless articles, books, programs, and the like published on this new generation of people. Unlike our parents, who raised us in the 70's and 80's, we are not satisfied unless we have it all. We want to be educated, compensated, promoted, and blessed with children at a point in our lives when we can actually afford full-time daycare without going into debt. We want our sons and daughters to grow up with the confidence that we have, and yet, not feel left behind when we scurry off to work at 7 a.m. each morning.

Because of these high aspirations we set for ourselves, I feel that I now work harder and play harder than ever before. Being thirty changes not only your perspective on life but enhances your responsibilities. My time is the most important aspect of my day, and I spend hours each week planning how to use it. Thirty is when the focus changes. I am now old enough to not rely on my parents for anything, and being a parent myself, have a little one who wants my time, money, and attention.

When I have a few moments to myself, I sometimes think back to those younger years when I did not know what I wanted in life. My parents supported me. I had much more free time and not much responsibility. Life was pretty good. It is even better at thirty.

CHAPTER 8

# *Whiff*

*You are never too old to set another goal or to dream a new dream..." —C.S. Lewis*

HAS YOUR BRAIN ever been hijacked? I imagine every single one of us can think of a time when we were embarrassed, confused, or bursting at the seams with frustration when something or someone caused every single cell of our brains to focus on that one negative thing. It takes us over and brings us down fast.

Write down those hijacked moments below.

_____

_____

_____

_____

The first time you pick up a golf club and take a swing at a ball might trigger this same response. When your response to a negative behavior overtakes your emotions, it is nearly impossible to reverse the outcome. If you start off with a whiff on your first swing, more whiffs are sure to follow if you do not recognize the signs that your brain has been hijacked and get it back on track.

*Emotional Intelligence* author Daniel Goleman offers a refuge to this hijacking by looking for ways to fuel the left frontal cortex of your brain. "Not all limbic hijackings are distressing," says Goleman. "When a joke strikes someone as so uproarious that their laughter is almost explosive, that, too, is a limbic response."

By identifying those things that trigger your emotional hijacking, you can retrain yourself to elicit neutral or even positive responses that don't overtake your brain for the moment, or even the entire day. How can you get started with this retraining process?

_____

_____

_____

*Take time off to restore*

What if you could hit an imaginary "pause" button at any time throughout your day to just take a breath and refocus? The reality of life is, that you can hit the "pause" button whenever you like, but many of us do not give ourselves permission to do so. As a parent, I use time-out as a disciplinary action for my kiddos when they get out of line. I need to reverse the roles sometimes and give myself a time-out when I start to tip towards the negative.

A good friend of mine shared with me her commitment to her workout routine. She said, "make an appointment on your calendar, just like you would for a work meeting and stick to it." If the time is blocked off where you can see it, and it is a standing appointment, you will find yourself committing to it. I have always thought it was sad that I have to schedule time off for myself. I do not mean vacations, but the small amounts of time that need to happen daily or at least weekly to rejuvenate. I always find excuses for why I do not have time to take even 15 minutes to relax (e.g. laundry needs folding, homework needs proofing, food needs to be prepared, and on and on). When I schedule the time and stick to it, my brain gets an instant recharge.

**CHAPTER 9**

# *The Back Nine*

"Golf combines two favorite American pastimes: taking long walks and hitting things with a stick." —P.J. O'Rourke

**THE FIRST TIME** I played golf as an adult — okay the first several times I played golf as an adult — I never thought I would see the end of the course. The clubhouse seemed miles and miles away, and my game got worse and worse. I was tired, my attitude was waning, and I kept asking "are we done yet?"

The beauty of golf, or any endeavor for that matter, is that the last half can push you into a winning state. Slow starters sometimes need to find their groove, and early achievers can leverage their momentum to coast on in. The back nine should be the downhill ride, but for some can be the uphill climb.

I have never understood why golf games take so long. To play eighteen holes takes, on average, four to five hours. That is longer than any other sport and most other activities (besides shopping — I could do that all day!). Why in the world would you want to torture yourself eighteen times if you are not playing well?

Here's my suggestion: only focus on nine of the holes. Golf courses are set up to provide players with both long and short holes and easy and difficult greens. No hole is the same, and sometimes, what appears to be the most daunting fairway can actually be your best play of the game.

If you focus on only nine holes, you can relax about the others. Any nine holes on a course will look and feel invariably different. What you will discover about yourself, and your golf game, is that when your mind is 100% focused on 50% of the task at hand, you will actually come out ahead.

I have a passion for home decorating. I get all giddy when turning on HGTV and marvel at the designers who take down walls and install new flooring, walls, and décor. I get a sparkle in my eye when looking around my own house and envision what could be. My biggest problem is that I do not paint very well, and my house is in pretty good shape.

To give my home's interior a little freshening, I decided to use some leftover paint to repaint my living room. Being the budget friendly gal I am (and also, I didn't want to fully admit to my husband that I wanted to spend money on hiring a painter), I prepped the space for paint. After moving furniture; taping off the trim, doors, and windows;

and getting the rollers and brushes out, I was ready to get started. Then I took a step back and decided where to begin.

It was at that point that I realized that my living room walls merged right into the kitchen walls. They also merged right into the front entryway and into the hallway leading to the bedrooms. What had started with just a little living room paint was looking like three to four rooms of painting. Whoa! Was that what I really wanted to do?

The project was a bit overwhelming to me at first. How much time was this entire project going to take, and did I really want to paint all those spaces?

With the prep-work taken care of, I took a deep breath and got started. I picked a corner of my living room as the start and worked my way around the room. After a couple of hours, I looked back at my progress, and was thrilled with the new paint color. It wasn't that much different from the former color of the room, but it had a fresh neutral palate that I could accessorize with anything. The feeling of creating a blank slate for the new treasures I would like to feature gave me the energy to forge ahead. In all, I painted the entire living room, hallway, and front entryway, and managed to merge the new paint color into my open kitchen while leaving the adjacent walls their original color. I did not have too many drips of paint on the trim work and only had to handle a few touch ups.

The most challenging part of my paint project was setting aside the time to do it. I knew if I tried to paint during the weekend days, my kids would either 1) want to help or 2) whine that I wasn't paying any attention to them. So, my solution was to paint at night. I am a stickler for getting a decent night's sleep, so I only gave myself two hours of painting time each night. When that two hours was up, I flipped on the ceiling fan, put my paint brushes in a Ziploc bag, and shuffled everything into the laundry room to be ready for the next night.

Subtle changes to your environment can strengthen your goal achievement process. *Success* magazine publisher Darren Hardy emphasizes the need to create positive habits in his book *The Compound Effect*. He encourages readers to do a little something each and every day that changes your behavior to produce a positive result. It is not the big changes that cause us to achieve success, but the small, seemingly insignificant decisions we make that move us forward.

> *"It's a funny thing, the more I practice the luckier I get"*
> —*Arnold Palmer*

What are some small things that you can do each day (think in 10-minute blocks of time) that can help change your behavior?

_____

_____

_____

_____

*The Back Nine*

I played sports in my youth. From the time I turned five until high school graduation, I participated in organized sports year round. I enjoyed the friendly competition, the camaraderie, and the friendships forged through years of structured exercise. I never really thought about the physical benefits that playing sports afforded me until I left home for college.

My high school graduation gift from my parents was a mountain bike. I was excited to take it with me to college as a means of transportation. I would not have a car with me my first year and thought a bike would get me where I needed to go. As I began my first semester at the University of Kansas, I quickly realized that the near 100-degree temperatures and a campus that sat on a hill were not the best circumstances for leisurely riding to and from class. Within the month, I had purchased a bus pass. My momentum for creating a physical activity out of my everyday needs was waning.

In addition to not having a car, I also entered college with no strings attached: no boyfriend and no best friend as my roommate. The very few high school classmates that also attended college with me were not in the same dorm, and I was barely acquainted with them. I was, in essence, starting from scratch with no expectations and lots of new beginnings.

*"The first half of your life is spent chasing success; the second half is spent chasing significance. There will be a time in your career, if it hasn't already arrived, when you'll begin to think about the legacy you'll leave behind. And suddenly the scraping and climbing you've been doing, and the energy you've spent trying to advance, will seem less important than the larger meaning behind your work and your life. If you start thinking in those terms now, you'll accomplish more, with greater satisfaction, than you thought possible. Don't wait until the end of your career to think about the meaning of your work."* —Cathie Black, *Basic Black*

**CHAPTER 10**

# *Power Play*

*"I never hit a shot, even in practice, without having a very sharp in-focus picture of it in my head." —Jack Nicklaus*

THE PURPOSE OF this book is to get you, reader, thinking in a way that gives you permission to embark upon activities and opportunities that may not appear to be socially acceptable. The beauty of how we approach life, is that we can create the rules. We have the power to decide how to engage with others, how to respond to threats, and most importantly, what doors we want to open and walk through.

The subtitle of this book: "What Men Know About Golf That Women Need to Master in Life" is no big secret. What men know is that golf is a metaphor for life. Golf is one, and only one, activity that creates an atmosphere of inclusion, socialization, permission, and opportunity that women have yet to fully embrace. I am not suggesting that you go out there and become a golf expert, but rather that you embrace the attributes that golf provides.

When Sheryl Sandburg published her New York Times Best Selling book *Lean In* in 2013, she was onto something. As the COO of Facebook, she walked the walk as a female executive each and every day. She understood the bias and created her own path out of what the new normal could be. She asked, "why not?" and went on to create the roadmap for many other women to follow. *Lean In* began a conversation on a topic that many of us were yearning to explore.

I am here to challenge you to create your new path. Whether that be the cart path or the path to establishing relationships that produce the results you desire. We are the creators and purveyors of our lives and success. Only we get to decide what works for us — whether it be on or off the golf course.

I will not be sad for a minute if you finish this book thinking that you still do not have a desire to pick up a golf club. My purpose here is not to create enthusiastic golf prospects, but to show you how a traditionally male sport doesn't always have to be that way. And more importantly, there are lessons to be learned from what men use the game of golf for.

> *"Mastering others is strength, mastering yourself is true power." —Lao Tsu*

The power play here is to gain power over our minds. That in itself is power. The power to believe in ourselves, the power to ask, "why not?" and the power to take action is ours. There isn't a rule book on how to live your life or build your career. The tools that I have shared with you from my own personal struggles and performance are, or I hope will be, a glimpse into how you can mold your life into one of significance and value.

The women that I have had the pleasure to meet and engage with in my life brought a significant amount of power to the table. Whether it is a powerful support role, or the powerful advocate standing up for herself, each and every one of us has a role in how we bring power to our lives and the lives of others.

I do have to share one last story, and that is the story of my grandma. She lived a most powerful life until the great age of 93. This slight woman, who barely reached the height of five feet tall, had a presence about her that commanded a room.

She liked to remind all of us that she grew up during the great depression, and that became her life-long mantra of "use it up, use it out, and make do with what you have." Upon graduating from high school, she took a job as a secretary in Panama. This would have been at the end of World War II, and pretty adventuresome for a young lady boarding a plane for the first time and heading to another country by herself.

The letters she wrote to her love (my grandpa) during this time were endearing. They described days of hard work, meeting new people, and the adventures she experienced while living abroad. He wrote back to her, of course, and tried to match her spirited tales, but mostly told of the day to day activities that were his normal.

She returned from Panama the following year, married my grandpa, and became a mother of three (the eldest being my mother). She became a homemaker with gusto. She had the drive and ability to become the CEO of any company, but decided her passion was to be the most powerful supporter of her husband through his career. Throughout her life, she never lost sight of what drove her: friendships, family, and community.

She was a community volunteer, even until months before her death when her health didn't allow her to participate. She cooked meals; visited the elderly; created a safe and warm home for her family and for the neighborhood; and donated her time, energy, and anything she had on hand to others in need.

She made things look easy. Her house was always amazing, with a fresh pot of coffee at the ready. She rarely left the house without her lipstick on and made many of her smashing outfits herself (including her wedding dress).

She was a spark of bright light that graced all of our lives and challenged us in ways that may have been frustrating at times, but always proved to be a life lesson. She asked the tough questions and held you accountable. She lived by example and offered you the opportunity to do the same. She was a fierce advocate not only for herself, but for those she loved. If she noticed something that was out of place (whether it be someone was left out or discriminated against), she was the first to speak up. I don't know if she knew what a powerful force she was, but that tiny woman played powerfully each and every day of her life.

I know that you have experienced someone powerful in your life. What does that look like? What attributes do they exhibit?

_____

_____

_____

_____

_____

_____

_____

*Golfing In Heels – Doing the Work*

The final section of this book is a way for you to dig a little deeper into how you can put into action the principles I have shared.

The power of visualization is a great start to creating the life and opportunities you desire.

What three things do you want for/in your life right now? Be specific — even write down the size, shape, color, dollar amount, and location…

I'll share a few examples:

I want to drive a white, luxury SUV with a leather interior, a sunroof, touch screen technology, and less than 50,000 miles on its odometer.

I want to weigh 145 pounds or less.

I want to make over $100,000 per year.

1._____

_____

_____

_____

2._____

_____

_____

_____

3._____

_____

_____

_____

How will you *feel* once you these things are in your life?

_____

_____

_____

_____

_____

What is standing in your way of getting these things?

_____

_____

_____

_____

_____

What is ONE thing you can do right now to take action toward achieving this goal/desire? And, this can be the smallest baby step. Is it research? Is it sharing your goal/desire with a loved one?

What is your new story? This one may take a little more time. So often, we create the stories in our minds about ourselves that we believe others have created for us. The power of you is that you can create your own story. I want you to use this space as a journal to write a new story about yourself. When you have achieved those goals, how will YOU describe yourself?

*"You have power over your mind – not outside events. Realize this and you will find strength."* —Marcus Aurelias

# Reading recommendations.

IF YOU HAVE come to the end of my book, thank you for reading it! I hope you are encouraged to seek out additional forms of motivation and research to keep you on your path to success. So many of the hurdles in my life have been overcome though the works of other authors. I want to share with you some of my favorite books, and the authors that have played a part in my journey. I hope you will check them out!

"The Success Principles" by Jack Canfield
- This book is a tried and true assessment of your life. I preferred to listen to it, versus reading it in print. Jack Canfield gets down to the baseline personal, family, career, and life goals that you are searching for.

"Girl, Stop Apologizing" by Rachel Hollis
- Rachel Hollis' second self-help book has taken her motivational prowess to the next level. This book will challenge you to find your own path and not apologize for who you are.

"High Performance Habits" by Brendon Burchard
- Brendon Burchard's story of getting raw with who he was meant to be creates a platform for performing at a higher level.

"Showing Up for Life. Thoughts on Gifts of a Lifetime" by Bill Gates Sr.
- This book, written by the father of Microsoft founder Bill Gates, tells the story of how the Gates family grew up and how life experiences, family, and deep friendships play a direct part in your success and overall life satisfaction.

"Switch: How to Change Things When Change is Hard" by Chip Heath and Dan Heath
- Chip and Dan Heath provide a hard look at how to make change within your organization. This work spoke to me at a time when I was stuck.

"The Four Agreements" by Don Miguel Ruiz
- These are basic mantras for how to live your life. It is a quick read, but makes you think about what you are saying to yourself and to others and about how you show up in the world.

*Reading recommendations.*

"Daring Greatly" by Brene Brown
- Get into the arena with Brene! She will walk you through how to give yourself permission to fly!

"The Seven Spiritual Laws of Success" by Deepak Chopra
- Mr. Chopra embraces the core of how we are meant to live. It is more than career success and can be applied to any belief system.

"Lean In" by Sheryl Sandburg
- The COO of Facebook is a women trailblazer extraordinaire! Learn about her experiences as an expectant mother working in Silicon Valley and asking for what all women need in the workplace.

"Different. Escaping the Competitive Herd" by Youngme Moon
- What sets you apart? And how do you even identify what that is?

"Mile Markers: The 26.2 Most Important Reasons Why Women Run" by Kristin Armstrong
- Even if you are not a runner, Kristin Armstrong's book provides motivation about life, parenting, friendships, and hard obstacles.

www.ingramcontent.com/pod-product-compliance
Lightning Source LLC
Chambersburg PA
CBHW071503080526
44587CB00014B/2198